Lewis and Clark for Kids

Their Journey of Discovery with 21 Activities

JANIS HERBERT

CHICAGO
REVIEW
PRESS

LIBRARY OF CONGRESS CATALOGING-IN-PUBLICATION DATA

Herbert, Janis, 1956–
    Lewis and Clark for kids : their journey of discovery with 21 activities / Janis Herbert.
        p. cm.
    Includes bibliographical references and index.
    Summary: An account of the Lewis and Clark expedition sent by President Jefferson
to explore the land acquired in the Louisiana Purchase in 1803. Includes related activities.
    ISBN 1–55652-374-2
    1. Lewis and Clark Expedition (1804–1806)—Juvenile literature. 2. West
(U.S.)—Discovery and exploration—Juvenile literature. 3. Lewis and Clark Expedition
(1804–1806)—Study and teaching—Activity programs—Juvenile literature. 4. West
(U.S.)—Discovery and exploration—Study and teaching—Activity programs—Juvenile
literature. [1. Lewis and Clark Expedition (1804–1806) 2. West (U.S.)—Discovery and
exploration.] 1. Title.
F592.7 .H38 2000
917.804'2—dc21

                                                                        99–048178

Front cover: *Map of Lewis and Clark's Track across the Western Portion of North America, from the Mississippi to the Pacific Ocean.* Courtesy of the National Archives. Meriwether Lewis and William Clark, Charles Willson Peale, 1807. Courtesy of Independence National Historical Park, Philadelphia, PA. *Four Bears (Mato-Tope), a Mandan chief.* Karl Bodmer, 1833–34. Courtesy of the National Archives. *Lewis and Clark at Three Forks.* Edgar S. Paxson. Mural in the Montana State Capital. Courtesy of the Montana Historical Society. *Source of the Columbia River.* Henry James Warre. Courtesy of the Denver Public Library.

Back cover: *Into the Unknown*, J. K. Ralston, 1964. Jefferson National Expansion Memorial. Courtesy of the National Park Service.

© 2000 by Janis Herbert
All rights reserved
First edition
Published by Chicago Review Press, Inc.
814 North Franklin Street
Chicago, IL 60610
1-55652-374-2
Printed in Singapore
5 4 3 2 1

To Mom and Dad, my adventurous, loving, and "honored parence"

Acknowledgments

This book was created with the gracious assistance of Betty Brill, Arabelle and Rose Britton, Sara Dickinson, Helen Waisanen, and Jason Williams. Many thanks to all of the people at Chicago Review Press, especially to editor Cynthia Sherry and project editor Rita Baladad, for their enthusiasm and devotion to this book. My thanks also go to Tamra Phelps for the book's beautiful design. With thanks, again and always, to Ruth and Don Ross, and to my supportive, wonderful husband Jeff.

Note to Readers

Warning—bad "speling" ahead! Throughout this book, you'll see quotes from Lewis's and Clark's journals that include some "creative" spelling and punctuation. The captains' education was not as formal as ours is today. Clark had very little schooling. But though they spell "mosquito" 20 different ways, their descriptions of people and landscapes show the captains' great intelligence and powers of observation. Please overlook their spelling errors and see the glossary for explanations of any other unfamiliar words in the text.

Contents

Time Line

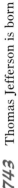

1743 Thomas Jefferson is born

1770 William Clark is born

1773 Boston Tea Party

1774 Meriwether Lewis is born

1775 Revolutionary War begins

1776 Continental Congress adopts Declaration of Independence

1783 Revolutionary War ends

1788 U.S. Constitution is ratified; George Washington is elected president

1789 Clark joins militia

1792 Captain Robert Gray enters Columbia River

1794 Whiskey Rebellion; Lewis joins militia

1800 Jefferson is elected president

1801 Lewis becomes President Jefferson's secretary

1802 President Jefferson asks Lewis to command an expedition to the west

1803 Louisiana Purchase. Lewis invites Clark to join him in command of the expedition

1804 President Jefferson is reelected; Vice President Aaron Burr kills Alexander Hamilton

1804–1806 Lewis and Clark expedition

1805 Louisiana Territory is formed

1807 Lewis is appointed governor of Louisiana Territory and Clark is appointed brigadier general of militia and superintendent of Indian affairs, Louisiana Territory

1809 Lewis dies

1812 War of 1812

1813 Clark is appointed governor of Missouri Territory

1814 The journals of Lewis and Clark are published

1826 Jefferson dies

1838 Clark dies

LEWIS AND CLARK at ST. CHARLES · MAY

Preface

To the Westward

Thomas Jefferson was born in Albemarle County, Virginia, in 1743. His father was a surveyor and planter. Thomas's mother was from one of Virginia's most distinguished families. Their tall, freckle-faced son grew up to become the third president of the United States. Jefferson wrote the Declaration of Independence and served as minister to France and later as secretary of state under President George Washington. In addition, he was an architect, naturalist, gardener, and inventor.

Jefferson designed and started building his elegant home, Monticello, when he was 26 years old. He conducted the country's first archaeological survey and found the bones of ancient Indians.

Jefferson also collected a great library and created the University of Virginia. By making the Louisiana Purchase and appointing the expedition to explore North America, he changed the face of the nation. Jefferson died on July 4, 1826, the 50th anniversary of the signing of his Declaration of Independence.

1803
Louisiana Purchase

"Honored Parence," wrote John Ordway, "I am now on an expidition to the westward, with Captain Lewis and Captain Clark, who are appointed by the President of the United States to go on an expidition through the interior parts of North America. We are to ascend the Missouri River with a boat as far as it is navigable and then to go by land, to the westward ocean. . . . I will write next winter if I have a chance. Yours, John Ordway, Sergeant."

Ordway wrote to his honored parents in May 1804 from a campsite in Illinois country, north of the frontier town of St. Louis. His letter may have made his family uneasy. The expedition he described was about to set off for an indefinite period of time over an uncertain course through wild and unmapped lands. Ordway was a member of the Corps of Discovery, the expedition of Lewis and Clark. This group of handpicked men was about to venture across the unexplored west of the American continent.

In 1800, the settled regions of the United States ended at the Mississippi River. In the western territories that would eventually include the states of Ohio, Indiana, and Illinois, a smattering of new settlers lived in windowless log cabins, dressed in deerskin, and hunted and farmed. Farther west was a vast, unexplored wilderness peopled by scattered Indian tribes. Only a handful of fur trappers had dared to travel beyond the great waters of the Mississippi River.

The United States was a young country, having only recently won its freedom from England. Starting as a small number of states along the eastern edge of the continent, the United States expanded south and west. Settler families broke the land

and built homes in the wild forests of Kentucky and Georgia. As the country grew, it pushed against lands claimed by other governments. Spain held the land now known as the state of Florida. It also held a vast area from the mouth of the Mississippi River north, including all the lands through which the Missouri River and its tributaries flowed. The land was called the Louisiana Territory. No one really knew how big it was—the vast region was unexplored by Europeans. In 1800, Spain relinquished the Louisiana Territory land to France.

In 1803, President Thomas Jefferson bought the territory from France. The Louisiana Purchase cost a fantastic sum—$15 million. The president knew it was money well spent. He had a vision of a United States that would someday span the continent. For now, however, he didn't even know how much territory he'd acquired. Where was the source of the Missouri River? How far did this new land reach? What mountains and forests did it hold? What people lived there and how did they live? Was it possible to reach the great Pacific Ocean by traveling along the course of the Missouri River? Jefferson had a passion for science and nature that made him even more curious about the new land. He wanted to know everything about the animals and plants, the climate, and the geography of the west.

Jefferson's many questions could only be answered by sending an exploratory party across the continent. It would be a dangerous, grueling, and challenging passage, perhaps an impossible one. Only the most courageous, resourceful, and devoted people could even attempt such a journey. Who would it be?

Thomas Jefferson

A Big Real Estate Deal

The territory of the Louisiana Purchase turned out to be 800,000 square miles in area. The $15 million Jefferson spent on the Louisiana Purchase came to three cents per acre and doubled the size of the United States!

1804

MAY 14   Lewis and Clark enter the Missouri River

MAY 21   The Corps of Discovery leaves St. Charles and embarks on its journey

AUGUST 20   Sergeant Floyd dies

AUGUST 30   The expedition holds council with the Yankton Sioux

SEPTEMBER 7   The men hunt for prairie dogs

SEPTEMBER 25   The expedition encounters the Teton Sioux

OCTOBER 8–12   The expedition stays with the Arikara

OCTOBER 25   The expedition reaches the Mandan and Hidatsa villages and searches for a site for its winter fort

NOVEMBER 4   Toussaint Charbonneau and Sacagawea join the expedition

1805

FEBRUARY 11   Sacagawea gives birth to Jean Baptiste "Pomp" Charbonneau

APRIL 7   The expedition leaves Fort Mandan and part of the expedition returns to St. Louis

APRIL 26   The Corps reaches the junction of the Yellowstone and Missouri Rivers

JUNE 2   The Corps reaches the junction of the Missouri and Maria's Rivers

JUNE 13   Lewis and his companions discover the Great Falls of the Missouri River

JULY 18   The Corps of Discovery passes through the Gates of the Rocky Mountains

JULY 25   The Corps reaches the Three Forks of the Missouri River

AUGUST 8   Sacagawea recognizes Beaver's Head Rock, a sign that the Corps is near the home of the Shoshone

AUGUST 13   Lewis meets the Shoshone

Lewis and Clark Expedition

AUGUST 17 Clark's party joins Lewis and the Shoshone; Sacagawea is reunited with her brother

AUGUST 18 Happy Birthday, Lewis!

SEPTEMBER 1 The Corps begins crossing the Bitterroot Mountains

SEPTEMBER 9 The Corps reaches Travelers' Rest

SEPTEMBER 20 The Corps meets the Nez Perce

OCTOBER 16 The Corps reaches the Columbia River

NOVEMBER 7 "Ocian in view!" Clark sees land's end in the distance.

NOVEMBER 18 The Corps sees the Pacific Ocean

NOVEMBER 24 One person, one vote: the Corps votes on where to camp for the winter

1806

DECEMBER 7 The Corps begins building its winter quarters, Fort Clatsop

MARCH 23 The Corps leaves Fort Clatsop and the return journey begins

MAY 11 The Corps reunites with the Nez Perce

JUNE 10 The Corps sets off to cross the Bitterroot Mountains

JULY 4 Back at Travelers' Rest, the Corps separates into smaller parties

JULY 25 Clark carves his name on Pompey's Tower

JULY 27 Lewis and his men fight with the Blackfoot

AUGUST 12 Lewis and Clark reunite at the junction of the Missouri and Yellowstone Rivers

AUGUST 14 The Corps returns to the Mandan and Hidatsa villages

SEPTEMBER 21 The Corps reaches St. Charles

SEPTEMBER 23 The Corps is back in St. Louis

Map of the Expedition

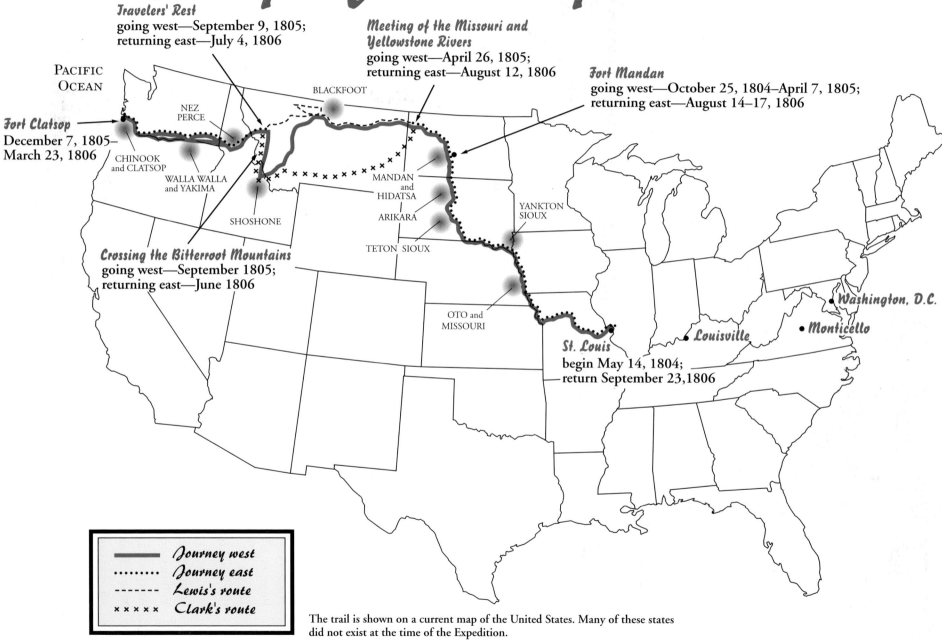

Travelers' Rest
going west—September 9, 1805;
returning east—July 4, 1806

Meeting of the Missouri and Yellowstone Rivers
going west—April 26, 1805;
returning east—August 12, 1806

Fort Mandan
going west—October 25, 1804–April 7, 1805;
returning east—August 14–17, 1806

PACIFIC OCEAN

BLACKFOOT

NEZ PERCE

Fort Clatsop
December 7, 1805–
March 23, 1806

CHINOOK and CLATSOP

WALLA WALLA and YAKIMA

SHOSHONE

MANDAN and HIDATSA

ARIKARA

TETON SIOUX

YANKTON SIOUX

Crossing the Bitterroot Mountains
going west—September 1805;
returning east—June 1806

OTO and MISSOURI

Washington, D.C.

Louisville

Monticello

St. Louis
begin May 14, 1804;
return September 23, 1806

Journey west
Journey east
Lewis's route
Clark's route

The trail is shown on a current map of the United States. Many of these states did not exist at the time of the Expedition.

xvi

1

Fixing for a Start

Meriwether Lewis and William Clark were born before the United States was a nation. In the year of Clark's birth, British troops fired into a crowd in Boston. Around the time of Lewis's birth, the colonists rebelled with the Boston Tea Party and Daniel Boone blazed a trail from the east to the far-off land of Kentucky.

1770
William Clark is born

1774
Meriwether Lewis is born

When Thomas Jefferson became president, he wrote to a trusted young friend and asked him to be his personal secretary. Meriwether Lewis was honored by the request.

Lewis was born in 1774, at a place very close to Jefferson's family home in Albemarle County, Virginia. Like President Jefferson, he was a planter's son. When Meriwether was just a young boy, his father, Lieutenant William Lewis, fought with George Washington against the British in the Revolutionary War. Meriwether rarely saw his father, so it must have been a special time when Lieutenant Lewis came home to visit in the fall of 1779. Sadly, when Meriwether's father left to rejoin the army, his horse fell while crossing a flooded and raging river. Lieutenant Lewis swam ashore and made his way back to his family's home, wet and bitterly cold. He developed pneumonia and died. Meriwether's mother remarried, and her new husband moved the family to Georgia, where they made a home in the wild, wooded country.

From a very early age, it seemed as if Meriwether Lewis was destined to become a great explorer. He was curious and fearless, and he loved to roam. Barefoot, with his eager dogs at his side, he tramped through the woods surrounding his family's Georgia home. The land was rich with wildlife, and on their walks the light-haired, blue-eyed boy and his dogs surprised deer and birds, and even an occasional black bear. By age eight, Lewis was skilled at fishing and hunting. Late at night he roused his dogs and went hunting for opossum and raccoon. When Lewis was nine, he was already so brave and confident that when he was charged by a crazed bull he held his ground, raised his gun, and shot the animal.

Lewis's mother, Lucy, taught him about the wild plants and trees surrounding their home. Lucy knew everything about how plants could be used as medicine, and she taught her young son how to recognize the plants and use them to treat illnesses. From her, Lewis also inherited a love for learning. Lucy's books were the most precious objects in their home.

Though he loved tramping around the woods of Georgia, Lewis wanted an education. As the oldest boy in his family, he knew it would someday be his responsibility to take over his father's plantation. He also had a natural curiosity about the world and was eager to learn. Because there were no public schools at that time,

Meriwether Lewis

Lewis set out to find a tutor. At age 13, he returned alone to Virginia and lived with a teacher.

Lewis poured himself into his studies. He learned grammar, "figurs" (math), geography, botany, and history. He read great books, poems, and plays. More than anything, Lewis loved to read the journals of Captain James Cook, a British navigator who explored the Pacific and Antarctic Oceans.

When he had time, Lewis stretched his long legs on hikes to the mountains of Virginia or to his mother's home in Georgia. He grew into a tall, handsome young man. Moody and somewhat shy, he felt more comfortable alone in the wild.

Lewis wanted to see the world and wanted to continue his education, but after five years of schooling he received a letter from his mother asking for his help. Her husband had died and she wanted to come back to Virginia. At age 18, Lewis moved his mother, brothers, and sisters back to his family's home in Virginia and became the head of their 2,000-acre plantation.

Lewis worked hard at managing the estate. He saw that the crops were planted and harvested, directed all the daily tasks, and planned for his family's future. His days were full, but the life of a plantation owner was not for him. Lewis was restless. Whenever he had time, he rode his horse far and wide or tramped on foot all over the countryside.

When Lewis turned 20, word spread throughout the country of a rebellion in the west. President Washington called for a militia (volunteer soldiers) to bring an end to the Whiskey Rebellion, and Lewis couldn't resist the urge to join up.

The long march over the Allegheny Mountains, from his Virginia home to western Pennsylvania, and the nights camping under stars agreed with Lewis. When the Whiskey Rebellion ended, he signed up for the regular army. "I am quite delighted with a soldier's life," he wrote his mother. He served as ensign under General "Mad Anthony" Wayne, who had gotten his name because of his reckless bravery during the Revolutionary War. (Wayne had led his soldiers against an alliance of Indians at the Battle of Fallen Timbers in the territory of Ohio. The treaty signed after that battle opened the land for settlers from the United States.)

Lewis became army paymaster. He traveled up and down the Ohio River on a large, flat-bottomed boat (called a keelboat), visiting different forts. For a time, he was assigned to the Chosen Rifle Company, an elite company of sharpshooters. The tall, red-headed captain of that company became a good friend of his. The captain's name was William Clark.

The two men had much in common. Clark was born in 1770 only a few miles away from Lewis's family home. Clark's father was a planter also. Lewis and Clark easily could have been childhood playmates. But while Lewis was shy and sometimes gloomy, Clark was friendly and outgoing.

Clark was the ninth of 10 children. When the Revolutionary War began, six-year-old Clark watched as his five older brothers rode off to fight the British. His oldest brother never came home again; he died as a British prisoner. Another brother, George Rogers, was a great hero of the war and close friend of Jefferson. His actions in battle secured the land that would someday become the states of Illinois, Kentucky, and Tennessee. Young

The Whiskey Rebellion

The Whiskey Rebellion of 1794 was an uprising against the new government by the grain farmers of Pennsylvania. A tax on whiskey upset the farmers, whose chief product was whiskey. One of their first protests ended comically. When 2,000 angry farmers marched against a U.S. fort in Pittsburgh, the people of the town gave them so much whiskey that the farmers were soon too drunk to do any damage. But when tax officials were tarred and feathered as they tried to collect taxes, President Washington took action. He called for a militia to put down the rebellion. The militia's appearance was enough to bring the revolt to a quick end. Though it doesn't seem like much now, at the time, the Whiskey Rebellion was a serious threat to the authority of the new government of the United States.

William Clark must have been tremendously proud of his heroic brothers.

When Clark was 15 years old, his family settled in the frontier land of Kentucky. The family built a log house, and Clark's father carved a plantation out of the wilderness. There were no towns, no schools, and very few neighbors in the new land. Clark wasn't able to get any formal education. He learned to read and write at home, and his brothers took the time to teach him about history, philosophy, and science. Clark, like Lewis, spent long hours tramping through the woods, hunting, and fishing. Out in Kentucky, in addition to being wary of bears and other wild animals, young Clark had to stay on the alert for Indians. The Indians who had lived here for so long were threatened by the new settlers and waged war against them. One of Clark's brothers was killed when Indians attacked the new settlement.

When Clark was 19, he followed in his brothers' footsteps and joined the military. He rose to captain, serving under Mad Anthony Wayne. When Lewis joined Clark's company, they quickly became friends. The two men saw in each other a trustworthy and honest companion. Lewis served in Clark's company for six months.

In 1796 the Indian wars in Ohio ended and Clark retired from the army. He was 26 years old and anxious to start a new life. He had learned a lot about the Native American people while he served in the army, and had great respect for Indian ways.

William Clark

He also had a passion for the wilderness. He wanted a life of adventure. He made a plan to travel up to the northern reaches of the Mississippi River and establish trade with the Indian tribes there.

Clark's plans were thwarted when he reached home. His brother, George Rogers, had fallen on difficult times, and Clark set aside his own dreams to help his brother get back on his feet. A few years later, their father died and Clark inherited a great deal of land in Kentucky. Instead of being free to pursue a life of adventure, he was tied to a large Kentucky plantation.

Lewis, in the meantime, remained in the army. He enjoyed traveling as army paymaster. In December 1800, he was promoted to captain. Then two months later he received the letter that would change his life forever.

1800
Jefferson is elected president

1801
Lewis becomes President Jefferson's secretary

Jefferson was about to be inaugurated as president of the United States. He needed an assistant, someone trustworthy and intelligent. Lewis fit the bill. His military experience and contacts would be of great help to the president. Jefferson wrote to Lewis and asked him to join him "as one of my family," to live at his house and help him with all the duties he would take on as president of the country. Lewis replied that he would "with pleasure accept the office." He took leave from the army and set out immediately for the capital in Washington.

For the next two years, Lewis lived and worked in the president's house. He was the president's right-hand man, helping him with all the duties of running the government. He even delivered President Jefferson's State of the Union address to Congress. (The president hated giving speeches!)

For years President Jefferson had thought about the lands to the west of the Mississippi River. Many countries were trying to lay claim to them. Spain, France, England, and Russia had all raised flags on some portion of North America. President Jefferson dreamed of a United States that would reach across the continent and hoped to stop these other countries from colonizing the western lands. The first step toward his dream would be to explore the length and breadth of the land. Even before the Louisiana Purchase, he wanted to send an expeditionary force to the west to find out about these unknown lands and report back on their discoveries. He hoped such an expedition would find a water route to the Pacific Ocean that would prove useful as a future trade route. Also, President Jefferson had a scientist's curiosity. What was out there in the western lands? What undiscovered peoples, animals, and plants? He thought about it constantly.

1802
President Jefferson asks Lewis to command an expedition to the west

In 1802 President Jefferson offered a challenge to his young assistant. Would Lewis lead an expedition through the unknown lands of the west? Lewis was the perfect choice. He was a skilled outdoorsman, brave and clear-headed. He had great strength of character, intelligence, and curiosity. Jefferson was confident that Lewis, now 28 years old, had all the qualities required for such a great challenge and would prove to be an outstanding leader for the expedition.

It was decided. Lewis would lead a corps of men up the length of the Missouri River, scaling any mountains along their path, which would end at the continent's edge. On the way, he would study and make notes of the climate, animal and plant life, and the presence of minerals. He would collect specimens of plants and animals for President Jefferson. He would meet with the Indian tribes who lived along the route, study their

Thomas Jefferson

Packing for a Long Journey

What would you take if you were about to set off on a journey through an unknown land for an indefinite length of time? You might want to pack your Nintendo, but you'd be better off bringing fishhooks. Lewis's list included warm clothes, lots of food, weapons, tools, and scientific instruments. He brought gifts for the Indians they would meet—tomahawks and tobacco, beads and bells, and vials of vermilion (red dye for face paint). He brought oiled cloth to serve as sails by day and tents at night, mosquito netting, candles, axes, medicines, hooks, kettles, and saws. He brought muskets and gunpowder. (The gunpowder was stored in recyclable packaging: it was packed in lead containers that kept it dry. As each container became empty, it was melted down and made into bullets.) There was a cannon for the boat and a special air gun that could fire without powder. Lewis had the food (dried "portable" soup, meat, and flour) packed in barrels. And, very important to this journey's mission, he brought lots and lots of ink and paper.

customs and languages, and speak with them about the new U.S. government in the east. He would map the vast area the expedition would cover, from the mouth of the Missouri River to the Pacific Ocean.

There were so many things President Jefferson and Lewis did not know about what lay ahead for the expedition. One thing they did know was that the expedition would have to travel a very great distance to reach the Pacific Ocean. In 1792 Boston seafarer Captain Robert Gray had rounded the Americas in his ship, the *Columbia*, and traveled far up the western coast of North America. He had reached a great river, which he named after his ship, and had calculated the river's location. By using special instruments and calculating the position of the sun and stars, Gray had pinpointed his position at the mouth of the Columbia River on the Pacific Ocean. With these measurements, President Jefferson and Lewis had a rough idea of the width of the North American continent—3,000 miles. Jefferson thought that the expedition would be able to travel by boat up the great Missouri River, make a short crossing overland to the Columbia River, then travel down the Columbia to the ocean.

It took Lewis a very long time to prepare for the journey. He had a lot of decisions to make. How many men should he take? The company should be large enough to accomplish its many tasks but not so large that it would look like a war party to the Native Americans they would meet. What supplies should he bring? He needed to feed and clothe the group for an undetermined (but definitely long) period of time. What kind of boat would they need? Lewis ordered a special keelboat constructed for the journey.

1803
Lewis invites Clark to join him in command of the expedition

Lewis's hands were full and his mind was bursting. There were so many tasks involved with getting ready for the expedition, to say nothing of the many things he would have to accomplish once it was underway. As he thought of the journey ahead, he came to the conclusion that it would require more than one commander. Lewis wanted a strong leader to help him command a corps of men through the vast west. This person would need to be a skilled woodsman who could help with the many challenges they would face in the wilderness, an equal partner who could take over all the tasks should something happen to Lewis. In June 1803, Lewis wrote a letter to the man he knew would fit the bill perfectly: his one-time commander, William Clark.

In his letter, Lewis described the nature of the expedition and the path it would take—down the Ohio River from Pittsburgh, Pennsylvania, to the Mississippi River, then up the Missouri River to its source. From there, Clark read, the expedition would travel by land to find the Columbia River,

where it would once again take to the water, following the river all the way to the Pacific ocean. It was the grandest, most exciting adventure Clark had ever heard of. He was thrilled when, at the end of the letter, Lewis asked him to join him in "its dangers and its honors." "There is no man on earth with whom I should feel equal pleasure in sharing them as with yourself," said Lewis. Clark replied immediately. "This is an undertaking fraught with many difficulties," he said. "But my Friend I do assure you that no man lives with whome I would perfur to undertake Such a Trip. I join you with hand and Heart." One of the most famous partnerships in history was formed. Lewis and Clark would serve as captains of the expedition to the west.

Lewis left Washington for Pittsburgh after receiving President Jefferson's instructions. Besides the main object of the expedition, to find a route to the Pacific Ocean, the explorers were instructed to measure latitude and longitude along the way and to draw maps of the country. They were to learn about the Indian tribes along the route, studying their languages, customs, and hunting practices. If any chiefs should wish to visit Washington, Lewis and Clark should arrange for them to come to the east. The captains were told to take careful notes of the climate and plant and animal life of the country they passed through.

Lewis spent long weeks in Pittsburgh waiting for his special boat to be finished. He grew more anxious every day to begin the journey. He hired several men who would help him take the boat down the Ohio River on the first leg of its journey. While he waited, he heard from Clark, who was waiting for him in the town of Clarksville, in Indiana Territory. Clark had been swamped with applications from young men who wanted to join them on their great adventure. He thought some were excellent young woodsmen. Lewis added a member to the expedition, too—a large, black Newfoundland dog he named Seaman.

After a long delay, the keelboat for the expedition was completed. Lewis had designed it, and it was named the *Discovery*. It was 55 feet long and 8 feet wide at its middle, tapering to 4 feet wide at the ends. It had a tall mast, and center poles that held up an awning. Eleven benches were made to seat 22 men at their oars. Its flat bottom would help it navigate shallow rivers. A cannon pointed out from the bow (the forward part of the boat), and a cabin was at the stern (the rear of the boat). Lewis also purchased another, smaller, boat, which was called a pirogue. (Pirogue is a French word for a flat-bottomed canoe made from a hollowed-out log.) And because Lewis knew that at some point in the journey they would have to leave the river and the keelboat behind, he had another special item built—a collapsible boat. It was a special lightweight iron frame that men could easily carry overland. Then when they got to water again, they could cover the frame with animal hides and turn it into a boat.

On August 31, 1803, Lewis and his men pointed the boats down the Ohio River. The trip down the river was miserable! The water was very low that summer, and every few miles the large keelboat got stuck on a sandbar. Sometimes Lewis and the men had to unload the boat to get it over the shallow places. Several times Lewis had to hire a local farmer with a team of oxen to tow the *Discovery* over sandbars. After several frustrating days, Lewis purchased another pirogue to carry some of the keelboat's load.

Lewis Joins the Club

In addition to packing and planning, Lewis had a lot of learning to do. President Jefferson wrote to scientists, scholars, and doctors, asking them to teach Lewis the skills he needed for the mission. Lewis examined the few maps that existed of parts of the Missouri River. He learned to recognize constellations. He learned how to calculate latitude and longitude. A doctor showed him how to treat medical emergencies. A botanist taught him how to categorize and preserve plants. An anatomist taught him about animals and fossils. Lewis learned everything he needed to know to fulfill the scientific part of his duties.

The scholars who taught Lewis were members of a special society formed by Benjamin Franklin. The American Philosophical Society was founded in 1743 and is still in existence. Thomas Jefferson and George Washington were among its first members; Lewis became a member, too. The focus of the society in its early years was natural history, including geology, astronomy, paleontology (the study of fossils), and the study of Indian cultures.

Big Bones

The discovery of the huge petrified bones of a woolly mammoth excited Lewis's imagination. He sent a box of the fossils back to President Jefferson. The site of the fossil discovery, called Big Bone Lick, was once a great marsh on the edge of the ice sheets that covered the North American continent 12,000 to 20,000 years ago. Animals that are now extinct, such as the woolly mammoth, the mastodon, the giant ground sloth, and a large relative of the buffalo, left their bones at this spot. Lewis, President Jefferson, and many scientists thought it was possible that these huge creatures still existed in the west, and that Lewis and Clark might meet some on their journey.

As they traveled downriver, the water became deeper and the way easier. The country here was less settled, and they saw fewer villages along the banks. They camped every night along the river's edge, sleeping heavily after the day's long work. One night, Seaman helped catch dinner. He swam into the river and caught squirrels as they were swimming across, then trotted to Lewis's side and laid them down. The men had fried squirrel that night.

One day they looked up to see huge flocks of migrating passenger pigeons. There were so many birds that they filled the sky! Another day they stopped to investigate the site of a recent discovery—the fossil bones of a huge mammoth. Eventually they arrived at Clarksville, where Clark was waiting for them. The two men were delighted to see each other again.

May 14, 1804
Lewis and Clark enter the Missouri River

Clark had done some preparations of his own while waiting for Lewis. He had interviewed dozens of eager young men who wanted to join the expedition. Clark and Lewis had agreed that they wanted brave and strong young men of good character. Hunting skills were very important. They also looked for men who had experience repairing boats, cooking, or making and repairing weapons.

When Lewis arrived, he and Clark chose a few of the many men who applied. They swore them into the army and into their expedition—the Corps of Discovery. Another new member of the expedition was Clark's slave York. York was the same age as Clark and had lived with him all of his life.

Soon they were back on the Ohio and rapidly approaching the Mississippi River. At one stop they met George Drouillard, a half-French, half-Shawnee fur trapper and scout. He spoke several Indian languages and was also skillful in the sign language used among the western Indian tribes. He was an excellent hunter and woodsman. Lewis and Clark asked him to join them on their journey and were happy when he said yes. As they continued to travel downriver, they stopped at army posts where other young men lined up for the chance to volunteer for the expedition.

Eventually they reached the junction of the Ohio and Mississippi Rivers. When they turned into the current of the mighty Mississippi River, the men learned just how hard it was to travel upstream. The sandbars of the Ohio seemed like nothing compared to the current of this powerful river. Pulling against the oars as hard as they could, they were able to travel only a few miles each day. They stopped at an army fort at Kaskaskia, where several soldiers volunteered to join them. They passed the frontier town of St. Louis, then reached Wood River, which they chose as their site for a winter camp. It was early December. They would go no farther until after the spring thaw.

The men quickly got to work cutting trees and building huts for their winter quar-

LEWIS AND CLARK *at* ST. CHARLES · MAY 21, 1804 ·

The Discovery in St. Charles

ters. They named their site "Camp Wood." Every day Clark lined the men up for military drill and shooting practice. Some of them weren't very good. When local settlers dropped by they held shooting contests with the explorers. The settlers usually won. It was a long winter, and the young men, who had signed up hoping for adventure, became bored and restless. They got into fights with one another. Some slipped out of camp and came back drunk.

Even though the stay at Wood River was tedious, it was a good way for Lewis and Clark to get to know the men and to choose those who would join them on the journey ahead. They couldn't afford to have any discipline problems on this expedition. They would only bring those men who showed good character, who could take orders and cooperate with others.

Lewis and Clark selected 26 men for the Corps of Discovery. These men would make the whole journey and would travel together on the keelboat. Another group of six soldiers, headed by Corporal Richard Warfington and paddling a pirogue, would accompany the Corps up the Missouri River for the first stage of the trip. After the expedition stopped for the second winter, this group would return south in the keelboat with the first batch of specimens and reports for President Jefferson. Eight French-Canadian voyagers would travel along in another pirogue and would return with Warfington's group.

The very best men were chosen for the Corps. Each had something special to contribute. Some were especially good woodsmen, some had experience with boats, and others were blacksmiths or carpenters. Two of the men, Pierre Cruzatte and Francis Labiche, were French-Indian traders who spoke Indian languages and had already traveled partway up the Missouri River. The rest of the men were glad to have Cruzatte and another private, George Gibson, along—they were great fiddlers. All the men were courageous, strong, hardy, and enthusiastic.

The weather began to warm. Snow melted and ice cracked, and the young men grew impatient to be on their way. Clark oversaw their work as they packed barrels and crates onto the boats. They were "fixing for a start," Clark wrote in his journal. Lewis went to St. Louis for last-minute errands and to send President Jefferson a package—containing tree cuttings and a horned toad! Finally, one gentle spring day in mid-May, they finished packing the Discovery and the expedition was ready to begin. The men pulled their oars and crossed the Mississippi River, then entered the mouth of the Missouri River. In two days of hard rowing, they went a short distance to the village of St. Charles; Lewis traveled from St. Louis on horseback and joined the boats there.

May 21, 1804
The Corps of Discovery leaves St. Charles and embarks on its journey

St. Charles, a rustic village of 500 people, was the last white settlement that the Corps would see for a very long time. In the morning, before they left, the men attended church. In the afternoon they were ready to set off. The villagers lined up along the bank and gave three cheers as the boats pulled away. On May 21, 1804, the men turned their backs on the world they knew and set their faces toward the west. Ahead lay adventure and an unknown land. In high spirits, the men pulled their oars against the Missouri River's strong current and their long journey began.

View on the Missouri

Where in the World Are You?
Learn about Latitude and Longitude

Globes and maps show the crisscrossing lines of latitude and longitude that navigators use to determine their location.

Latitude lines run horizontally (east and west) in parallel lines approximately 69 miles apart. (Because they run parallel to each other, these lines are called "parallels.") Each line is assigned a number, or "degree," from 0 to 90. The equator's number is 0 degrees. The North Pole's latitude is 90 degrees north; the South Pole's is 90 degrees south. These numbers are based on the concept that a circle has 360 degrees. If you walked from the equator to the North Pole, you would have made it one-fourth of the way around the circle that is earth. One-fourth of 360 degrees equals—guess what?—90 degrees!

Longitude lines (called "meridians") run vertically, or north and south. They meet at the poles and are farthest apart at the equator (where they are approximately 69 miles apart). Navigators decided that 0 degrees longitude would be at Greenwich, England. Longitude lines are evenly spaced around the earth 180 degrees east and west from Greenwich, and meet at a line in the Pacific Ocean called the International Date Line.

Pretend you're President Jefferson, sitting at your desk in Washington. "Mr. Lewis," you say, "I want you to take a long journey across the continent, all the way to the Pacific Ocean." "How far is that?" asks Lewis. "Well," you say, "Let me calculate. . . ."

Materials

- *Pencil and paper*
- *Globe or map that shows lines of latitude and longitude*

On the globe or map, locate the mouth of the Columbia River (at Astoria, Oregon). Locate Washington, D.C. What are the latitudes of these two locations? (For answer, see #1 below.)

ANSWERS:
#1: Columbia River: approximately 46 degrees north. Washington, D.C.: approximately 39 degrees north.

North ↕ South

West ←——→ East

Longitude

If each degree of latitude is 69 miles, approximately how many miles north of Washington, is the Columbia River? (See #2 below.)

What is the longitude of the two locations? (See #3 below.) How many degrees west of Washington is the Columbia River? If they were along the equator, how many miles apart would they be? (See

Latitude

#4 below.) Do you think the actual distance Lewis will travel will be shorter or longer than this? (See #5 below.)

Look for your own hometown and estimate its latitude and longitude. If President Jefferson summoned you to Washington, about how far would you have to travel to get there?

#2: 483 miles (46 degrees - 39 degrees = 7 degrees; 7 degrees x 69 miles = 483 miles).

#3: Columbia River: approximately 124 degrees west. Washington, D.C.: approximately 77 degrees west.

#4: 47 degrees (124 degrees - 77 degrees = 47 degrees); 3,243 miles (47 degrees x 69 miles = 3,243 miles).

#5: Shorter. The farther you are from the equator, the closer together the longitude lines are. So in the United States, the longitude lines are fewer than 69 miles apart.

Very Very Vermilion

ewis knew red face paint (called vermilion) would be a welcome gift among the Indians they would meet. His dye was made from grinding minerals into pigment. Here's an easier version.

Materials

- *1 tablespoon cornstarch*
- *½ teaspoon water*
- *1 tablespoon cold cream*
- *8 drops red food coloring*
- *Cup*
- *Spoon*
- *Paintbrush*

Stir the cornstarch, water, cold cream, and red food coloring together in the cup. Use the paintbrush or your fingers to paint your face with your own design. This dye stays damp on your skin. Once you paint it on, don't touch your face until you're ready to wash it off.

2

We Set Out Early

May 1804
The expedition navigates the muddy Missouri River

On the first night along the great river, the company camped on an island. Captains Lewis and Clark assigned men to stand guard, as they would throughout the length of the journey. That night and those that followed must have seemed all too short. When the sun came up, the men stretched their sore muscles and got ready for another day of battling the river's powerful current.

Rowing the boats on the Missouri River was like trying to ride a wild animal. The men were constantly on the alert as they fought their way upstream. The river's currents were swift and dangerous. One man sat in the bow of the keelboat to look for hazards ahead. The others rowed, pushed, and pulled upstream. If they couldn't make progress with their oars, they pushed long poles into the river's bottom to shove the boat forward. They used sails whenever there was a helpful wind. If that didn't work, they got out and tied ropes to the boat and pulled it along, splashing through the shallows close to the banks. The river was so full of soil that it was hard to see far into its muddy brown waters. As the men pulled the tow-

lines, their feet slipped on rocks. As they passed islands, whole banks would crash into the water and tons of earth would threaten to swamp their boats. Giant trees would suddenly come toward them, carried along on the water's surface.

There was never a moment when the river did not require their constant attention and labor. They made slow progress, averaging around 15 miles a day. Their poles broke and their oars snapped. One day the mast of the keelboat caught on a tree limb and snapped in two. They made frequent stops to repair the boats and equipment.

While most of the men pushed or pulled the boats upstream, the better hunters among them walked along the banks or rode two horses they had brought on the journey. They kept a sharp lookout for game. They hunted for deer, ducks, and geese to feed their companions. When they were successful, they hung the game on trees along the banks of the river for the boatmen to pick up as they went by.

On most days, Captain Lewis walked along the shore with his dog Seaman by his side. He made observations of animals and collected plants, looking especially for those that did not occur in the lands to the east. In his knapsack he kept a journal handy for drawings and descriptions. He also carried a compass, his rifle, and a long staff with a metal-

Preserving Plants

Lewis collected and preserved hundreds of plants, flowers, seeds, and cuttings. His collection became an important contribution to the science of botany. Some of the plants have been lost over the years, but many are still held by the Academy of Natural Sciences of Philadelphia. You can start your own museum collection at home.

Materials

- *Plant identification book*
- *Scissors*
- *Journal and pencil*
- *Lots of newspaper*
- *Spray bottle of water*
- *A large, wide board about the same size as a sheet of newspaper*
- *Four bricks or heavy books*
- *Heavy paper*
- *White glue*
- *Toothpick*
- *Tweezers*

Before starting your collection, ask permission to pick plants—some nature preserves don't permit collecting. Identify plants before touching them. Know what poisonous plants such as poison ivy and poison oak look like.

Bring damp newspaper along on your walk. After you've chosen and cut your plants, place them between the pages of the newspaper and gently roll the paper up. This will keep the plants fresh until you're ready to press them. Record in your journal what the plant looks like and the date and place where you collected it.

When you get home, unroll the newspaper. Lay 20 pages of dry newspaper on the floor in a place where you can let it stay for a few weeks. Arrange your plants on it. Cover with another 20 pages of dry newspaper. Place the large board over the paper and set the bricks on top of the board.

Every day replace all of the newspaper on the top and bottom with dry paper. Total drying time for the plants will take 20 days. Move the plants with tweezers every other day for the first 10 days. Let the plants dry for another 10 days without moving them.

Mount your plants on heavy paper. Pick up each plant with the tweezers and hold it. With a toothpick, place a tiny bit of glue on the back of the plant. Set the plant on the paper and gently press it down. Label the plant, including the date and place you picked it. Or fold the heavy paper into a note card and send it to a friend!

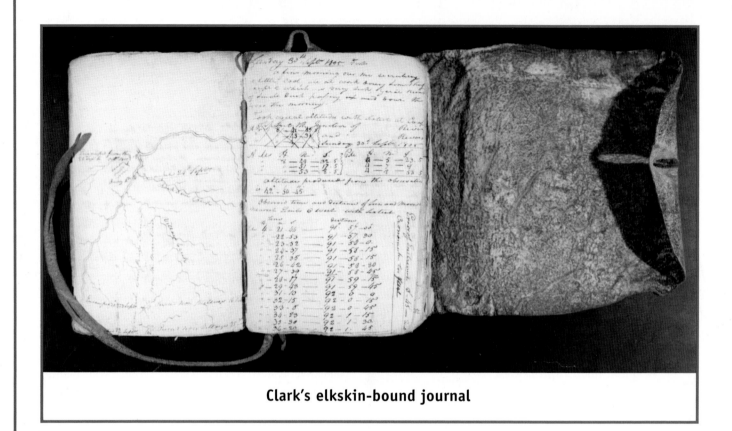

Clark's elkskin-bound journal

tipped spear called an "espontoon." This weapon usually served him as a walking stick, but once it saved his life. Early in the journey, Lewis climbed high up a cliff that towered above the river. Three hundred feet above the rocky shore he slipped and fell, saving himself just in time by thrusting his espontoon into the cliff face.

Lewis was excited by the new landscapes unfolding before him, and he enjoyed these solitary walks. By nature aloof, he found it a relief to be away from the group of men for at least part of the day. Clark, who was the more skilled boatman, stayed on the keelboat. He directed the men in their efforts,

and on a slate made careful notes of the twists and turns of the river. He used his notes later to make precise maps of the Missouri River. Clark was more comfortable with the men than Lewis, and this division of labor was agreeable to both of them.

Though they liked and respected each other tremendously, Lewis and Clark were very different from one another. The red-headed Clark was warm and even-tempered. He was well liked by the men, and at the same time he strictly maintained his role as commander. Lewis was more reserved. The men of the Corps had great respect for Captain Lewis but found him less friendly than Captain Clark.

Slowly the expedition progressed upstream. The days grew hotter and more humid. On some days, huge thunderheads filled the sky, and lightning and thunder crashed around them. After the storms passed through, the air was clear and fresh. Whenever possible they camped on islands at night, safe—they hoped—from animals and Indians. Clark described the country they went through as "rich and well timbered, abounding in Deer Elk & Bear," though "the Ticks & Musquiters are verry troublesome." At night mosquitoes swarmed their camps until it was nearly unbearable. The men covered themselves with grease and stood in the smoke of their campfires to drive away the insects.

When they stopped at the end of each day, Clark surveyed the land, noted geological formations and weather, and drew maps. He drew and named landmarks and the streams that flowed into the Missouri River—like Fourth of July Creek and Independence Creek (to honor their country's birthday) and Joseph Field's Snake Prairie for the place where one of the men

Fruit Leather

Dried fruit was a real treat and added necessary vitamins to the men's diets. Here's a recipe for dried fruit that you can take on your own expeditions.

Materials

- 2 apples, peeled and cut into small chunks
- 1 tablespoon lemon juice
- Blender
- Saucepan
- Spoon
- ¼ teaspoon cinnamon
- Cookie sheet
- Plastic wrap (or recycle—cut a small plastic bag and lay it flat)
- Tape

Adult help suggested.

Place the fruit and lemon juice in the blender and puree until smooth. Spoon the mixture into the saucepan and cook, stirring, over medium heat until it's thick (5 to 10 minutes). Remove from heat, add the cinnamon, and allow to cool. Line the cookie sheet with plastic, taping it down at the sides so it doesn't move. Spoon the mixture onto the plastic wrap. Spread it in a very thin layer with the back of the spoon. Set near a sunny window to dry for a day. Peel off and eat!

was bitten by a snake. Lewis took the temperature and made measurements of latitude and longitude. Together the captains made lunar observations and noted the positions of the stars.

The captains and some of the men kept journals during the journey. Sitting close to the campfire at night, they dipped their quill pens in ink and noted the day's events in their journals. "Set out early under a gentle breeze," "Broke our toe rope," "We proceeded on," and "A cool evening, two beaver caught today" were typical entries.

The privates pitched tents made of the boat's sails. They collected firewood and cooked the meat the hunters provided. George Drouillard was the best hunter of the group and brought in the most game. One day he brought down eight deer for the Corps. York had some knowledge of wild plants and he gathered greens for the men to eat. Seaman did his part and caught an occasional rabbit or bird. Any leftover meat was dried to eat another day. On days when the hunters were not successful, the men were given rations from the barrels on the keelboat. Because they didn't stop to cook during the day, they would prepare the next day's meals at night from the supplies of saltpork, ground corn, dried apples, and flour. They drank the muddy river water and made gritty coffee from it, too. (A glass of water taken from the Missouri River was half mud!) Occasionally, on days when they had worked especially hard, the captains would treat the men to a ration of whiskey. As the summer progressed they added berries to their meals, gathered from bushes along the banks of the river. They cleaned their weapons, which became rusty from river water and rain. They repacked their supplies and reloaded the boats. After their chores were done, Pierre Cruzatte

and George Gibson played their fiddles and the men sang loudly and danced rough dances. The campfires made small circles of warmth and light in the vast and empty wilderness.

One day, the expedition met a small group of fur trappers coming downstream as they were struggling upstream. These rough men were paddling downriver with their pirogues piled high with the pelts (hides) of animals they'd spent the winter trapping. Trappers stayed in the wilderness for months at a time, then brought their pelts to trading posts only to load up on supplies and go back out again.

One of the trappers was Pierre Dorion, a Frenchman, who had lived with the Sioux for 20 years and was married to a Sioux woman. When Lewis and Clark heard that he spoke the Sioux language, they asked him to join them as far as the Sioux villages that they knew were ahead to the north. The captains had heard that the Sioux were warriors. Dorion could help them communicate with this nation of Indians.

Up to this time, the men had only seen a small group of Kickapoo people and, from a distance, a hunting party of an unknown tribe. They did see several abandoned Indian villages and other signs of human presence. Huge mounds of earth rose along the banks of the river, mounds that could only have been built by humans. There were pictographs, or rock drawings, on cliff faces and in caves. But for the most part the landscape they passed through was empty of man, woman, or child.

The Missouri River began to curve from west to north, and the country changed from dense forest to open prairie. The land gently sloped to the water's edge, the soft, waving green grasses a con-

Imagine how hard it would be to identify an animal you had never seen before. You would probably start by comparing it to other animals that look the same. Coyotes look like wolves, and so do dogs. In fact, these animals are all closely related biologically—they all belong to the same family. However, sometimes appearances are deceiving. A bat and a robin might both have wings, but they are very, very distant relatives.

In the 18th century, the Swedish botanist Carolus Linnaeus developed the system of classification we use today. This system has seven different levels of classification. At the first level (kingdom)

It's a Phase—Learn the Lunar Cycle

Indians counted time by "moons," and our calendars, too, are based on the moon's monthly revolution around the earth. You can track time by observing the moon's phases as Lewis and Clark did.

The moon's light is reflected light from the sun—we can only see the parts of the moon that the sun is shining on. When the moon is between the earth and the sun, we can't see it (the sun is shining on the side that's facing away from us). During this phase, the moon is called the "new moon." Every day it shifts in its orbit around the earth. The day after the new moon, a tiny crescent of the sunlit moon is seen from the earth. Every day it appears bigger (we say it is "waxing"). It shows up right after sunset, then sets below the horizon.

A week after the new moon, the moon appears as a half circle. Then it's called the "first-quarter moon" because it's one-quarter of the way through its revolution. It's in the sky during the afternoon and evening and sets in the middle of the night. When the moon is greater than a half circle it's called a "gibbous moon". Halfway through its cycle, the moon is full. It rises at sunset and sets at sunrise.

The moon now begins to wane, or become smaller. It first becomes a gibbous moon, then a half-circle moon in its third quarter, when it rises in the middle of the night and sets around noon. In another few days it is a crescent. Finally it disappears. Once again it's a new moon and a new month. Here's a way to really understand how this works.

Materials

- *Lamp (with lampshade removed)*
- *Tennis ball*
- *Golf ball*

Pretend the lamp is the sun. The tennis ball will be planet earth and the golf ball the moon. Hold the earth in one hand and the moon in another.

For the first phase, or new moon, hold the moon between the earth and the sun. The side facing the earth is dark, just like the moon when it's new. Slowly move the moon in a circle, or revolution, around the earth and observe where the sun shines on the golf-ball moon. Even though it's a globe, an observer on earth would only see the parts of the moon the sun is shining on. As the golf-ball moon moves one-quarter of the way around the tennis-ball earth, the lamp sun shines on it so that a half-circle would appear to an observer on earth. Take a look! Complete the cycle around the earth and gain an understanding of lunar phases.

trast to the brown, churning river. Cottonwood trees lined the streams that flowed into the Missouri. The rest of the land was a vast and beautiful expanse of tall grasses and wildflowers. "Nature appears to have exerted herself," wrote Clark. The river wound through plains of prairie grasses five to eight feet high. Lewis happily collected seeds and cuttings from plants. He pressed and dried flowers and leaves to preserve them for President Jefferson's collections.

The hunters found plenty of game, and the men had geese, ducks, and wild turkeys for dinner. The boatmen caught giant catfish. Two brothers who were part of the Corps, Reuben and Joseph Field, caught a baby wolf. They hoped to tame it, but the little wolf chewed through the rope they had tied it with and escaped. At another time, Seaman dove into a beaver's lodge and drove its inhabitants out. One day the men caught an animal none of them had ever seen before. Clark wrote about it in his journal. Its short, powerful legs and long front claws were clues that this animal was a burrower. Clark also noted its small ears and the white stripe that ran from its nose all the way back over its head. The animal was a badger.

Another day they puzzled for hours over what looked like a huge white cloud on the surface of the river, far in the distance. As they drew closer, they realized it was a resting flock of birds that extended over three miles of the river. They were pelicans, thousands of them. Lewis shot one for a specimen, and the men were astonished by the marvelous bird. Its large pouch, which the pelican uses to scoop up fish, fascinated the men. They filled it with water and found that it could

hold five gallons! Another new animal barked at them from the banks of the river. In his journal, Clark described this animal, now known as the coyote. He called it a "Prarie Wolf."

August 3, 1804
The expedition meets Oto and Missouri people

Though they'd heard from fur traders about the great buffalo herds of the west, the members of the expedition still hadn't seen one. Perhaps that explained why they hadn't seen Indians yet either, for many of the tribes followed the herds. But one day in early August as they were making camp, the men were visited by a small group of Indians from the Oto and Missouri tribes. Settled, agricultural people, these tribes came to visit from villages nearby. Lewis and Clark invited them to bring their chiefs for a council the next day.

In preparation for the council, the captains dressed in their fanciest dress coats and three-cornered hats. The men made an awning from the sail of the keelboat. They constructed a flagpole and raised the U.S. flag over their camp. When the Indian chiefs arrived, they were given seats under the awning. The Corps performed military drills for them. Lewis gave a long speech, which was translated by a French trapper, telling the chiefs about the new country of the United States. He explained the purpose of the expedition's journey through the land and told them how President Jefferson hoped to build a road of peace between Washing-

plants are distinguished from animals, and both are distinguished from other organisms (like bacteria). Within each level after kingdom (phylum, class, order, family, genus, and species), organisms are classified in more and more specific ways.

We know that coyotes, wolves, and dogs are in the animal kingdom. The Linnaean system further places them in the:

Phylum *Chordata* (animals with backbones)
Class *Mammalia* (warm blooded, milk producing, and furry)
Order *Carnivora* (meat eating)
Family *Canidae* (doglike animals with four-toed hind feet).

The scientific names given to these animals come from the last two categories—genus and species. The coyote is *Canis latrans*; the timber wolf is *Canis lupus*. *Canis familiaris* is the scientific name for the domestic dog—the kind you might have as a pet.

A look at the human place in this system shows how closely related we are to other animals. You're in the same kingdom, phylum, class, and order as your family dog or cat. "Mitakuye oyasin," say the Lakota—"We are all related."

Court-Martial

The captains had chosen their men well. There were very few instances when a member of the Corps of Discovery needed to be disciplined. Everyone understood that the rules were made for the safety of the expedition. If one person stole food from the supplies, it might mean there wouldn't be enough for everyone later on the journey. Falling asleep at one's post at night could endanger everyone. Moses Reed tried to desert, an act punishable by death in the military of that time. Men who were charged with one of these acts were tried by a court-martial—a military court made up of other members of the Corps. The court-martial voted on guilt or innocence and decided the punishment. Whipping was a common punishment of the time.

ton and the lands of the people to the west. The captains gave the chiefs gifts of tobacco, dye, and gunpowder, along with peace medals—special medals issued by President Jefferson for just such a purpose. The chiefs listened quietly, spoke little, and thanked the captains for the gifts. To top off the occasion, Lewis demonstrated his special air gun for the astonished Indians. Clark named the place where they'd met with the chiefs Council Bluffs, in honor of the events of the day.

The expedition continued up the river, winding its way between large bluffs. One of the privates, Moses Reed, requested permission to go back to Council Bluffs. He said he'd lost a knife and wanted to retrieve it. The captains allowed him to go, but when he didn't return a few days later they suspected that he was trying to desert the Corps. When they brought Reed back, he admitted that he'd tried to run away and had stolen a gun and supplies. His actions had put the expedition in danger. The punishment for desertion from the army was death, but Captains Lewis and Clark instead sentenced Reed to "run the gauntlet" (that is, to run between two rows of men who struck him as he passed), and they removed him from the Corps of Discovery. Reed joined the men in the pirogue and would return to St. Louis when the party split up.

Soon the expedition passed Black Bird Hill, which overlooked a vista of rolling grasslands, clusters of trees, and a long view of the brown Missouri River. Black Bird, chief of the Omaha people, loved the view and had asked to be buried on this hill. When he died, his tribe placed him in full war costume with headdress and buried him on the back of his horse with a bow in his hand and a shield on his arm.

August 20, 1804
Sergeant Floyd dies

Shortly after passing Black Bird Hill, the Corps lost one of its own men. Sergeant Charles Floyd had been feeling sick for days. Captain Lewis tried every healing art. Floyd's comrades attended him carefully, with York paying special attention to the sick man. However, nothing seemed to help him. Floyd quickly grew worse and soon died. The men were saddened at the loss of their comrade, a young man, Lewis wrote, "of much merit." They buried him with military honors at the top of a bluff above the river. From here, like Black Bird's, Floyd's spirit could see the river and the country for miles around. Clark placed a cedar post above the grave of this man, who, Clark said, "at all times gave us proof of his firmness, and determined resolution to do service to his country, and honor to himself." In honor of Sergeant Floyd, the captains named a nearby stream for him—the Floyd River.

At a campsite days later, the Corps held an election to choose an officer to take Sergeant Floyd's position. Patrick Gass received the majority of the votes and was promoted to sergeant. A member of Warfington's group was given Gass's place as a private in the Corps.

It had been a difficult time, and that night they had another reason to worry. Private George Shannon, at 18 the youngest man in the Corps, had gone out hunting with the horses. Night had come on, and he hadn't returned. The captains were concerned about the boy all alone in the wilderness. Drouillard and Private John Colter were sent to look for Shannon, but he was nowhere to be found. After a time they had to move on, and they all hoped that wherever he was, Shannon was safe and would find them again.

The expedition passed high red bluffs that looked as if they had been on fire, and rowed upriver through a windstorm. They were entering the Great Plains, a vast expanse of nearly treeless prairie. The sky here seemed endless.

One landmark stood out, a high conical hill, and the captains spent a day investigating it. They'd heard the Indians' stories about this place, which

View from Floyd's grave

The Buffalo

At one time the American bison, commonly known as the buffalo, wandered over the plains in enormous herds. Some scientists think there were as many as 60 million buffalo at the time of the Lewis and Clark expedition. Herds of thousands blackened the land, some so big that if you stood in one place watching, it could take days for a single herd to pass.

The massive male buffalo stands six feet high at the shoulder, is 10 feet long, and can weigh up to 2,000 pounds. Females are about half that size. A buffalo's huge head, short neck, and humped shoulders are covered with brown shaggy fur, and a beard hangs down from its chin. The rest of its body is covered with a sleeker brown coat. Two short horns curve out from its forehead, and its small tail busily brushes away flies and insects.

Like the cattle they're related to, buffalo graze on grass. They survive the north's harsh winters by growing longer coats as cold weather approaches. They feed in winter by pushing at the snow with their great heads to get to the grass beneath.

During the mating season, males bellow and snort at each other and sometimes fight. They crash their heads together, or lower them and slam into their opponents from the side. Thirty- to 40-pound calves are born in the spring. For much of the year, the mother buffalo and their young stay together in small bands, and the bulls graze in groups of their own. They all join together in summer and early fall.

Many Indian tribes hunted buffalo. They not only ate the meat and used the animals' skin for clothing and tipis, they also made tools from buffalo bones and even used the tendons for bowstrings and thread.

White hunters and the coming of the transcontinental railroad reduced the population of these giant herds nearly to extinction. One hundred years after Lewis and Clark's journey, there were only a couple of dozen wild buffalo left in the whole United States! They have since been nurtured back from the brink of extinction, but they are not anywhere near their previous numbers. Small herds live in parks and preserves across the west.

was called Spirit Mound. It was said to be inhabited by large-headed, humanlike creatures only 18 inches tall. These creatures were supposed to be very jealous of their hill, and it was said that they would kill with their sharp arrows anyone who approached. Indians never went near it. Lewis and Clark, with some of the men and Seaman, disregarded the warnings and explored the hill that hot summer day. Seaman soon turned back to the camp to lie in the cool water of a nearby creek. The captains reached the top of the hill and tried to understand why the Indians avoided it. It stood strangely alone in the level plain. A very large number of birds gathered there and the wind that blew across the

Lewis and Clark crossing South Dakota

land seemed especially strong from the top of the hill. But they saw no large-headed creatures and suffered no harm. They hiked back to their camp.

The river took them through lands rich with wildlife. One day Private Joseph Field came rushing back from a hunt, running to the bank of the river and shouting for the men to bring the boats ashore. He had killed a buffalo. Within a couple of days, they saw herds of thousands of these magnificent animals on either side of them as they traveled upriver. The men marveled at the giant beasts with the huge shaggy heads.

Where buffalo were found, the captains thought, Indians couldn't be far behind. One day they lit a smoky fire as a signal announcing to any nearby tribes: "We are here." It worked. A few hours later several young Indian boys came to their camp. The French trader, Dorion, understood their language and learned from the boys that their band, of the Yankton Sioux nation, was nearby. The captains sent the boys back to their chiefs with gifts and an invitation to come to a council.

3

We Smoke the Pipe of Peace

The Branches of the Sioux Nation

The Santee Sioux lived near the Mississippi River. The Yankton Sioux occupied the plains east of the Missouri River. The seven tribes of the Teton Sioux lived west of the Missouri River. They are:

The Sihasapa (Blackfoot), named for their dark leggings and moccasins.

The Sicangu (meaning "Burned Thighs"), now known by a French version of that name, Bois Brule.

The Hunkpapa, who received their name from their status as great warriors. At tribal gatherings, this tribe guarded the entrance of the camp to guard against attack. Their name

Teton Sioux horse races

August 30, 1804
The expedition holds council with the Yankton Sioux

When the Yankton Sioux chiefs came to the expedition's camp, the captains once again dressed in their best. Lewis and Clark put on a military drill and gave a speech (which Pierre Dorion translated from English into the Sioux language). The chiefs, too, wore their finest apparel, ornamented with porcupine quills and eagle feathers. They carried shields of white buffalo hide. The captains named the meeting place Calumet ("peace pipe") Bluffs. After the council, they visited the Indian camp. As night fell, young Indian warriors danced in the flickering firelight to the steady beat of drums and rattles. The men of the expedition gave the dancers gifts of tobacco and knives.

A Hunkpapa Sioux

The captains had heard stories about the great Sioux nation. The Sioux traveled with the seasons and the buffalo herds. Expert riders, the people of this great tribe raced their ponies across the plains in pursuit of the immense herds. The gifts from the buffalo were many—food, clothing, and shelter. The people also gathered chokecherries and wild plums, and hunted for ducks, geese, and small game.

In these times, when a Sioux couple married, the young man went to live with his wife's family. Their babies were welcomed and taught by the whole community. As infants, they spent their first year wrapped snugly inside a cradleboard and carried on their mother's back. When they were young children, the whole village was theirs. In Sioux tradition, children were cherished and yet not overprotected. Never spanked and seldom reprimanded, Sioux children learned by watching and listening to their elders. Girls followed their mothers to learn how to pick the right herbs, to do quillwork, and to prepare buffalo hides; boys had small bows and arrows and imitated their fathers on the hunt. Stories told around the fire taught them their tribe's history and offered lessons on how to live.

As boys and girls grew into adulthood, they were sent off alone to fast and pray for a vision that would determine their life's path. A special animal might appear in a vision or dream, an animal that would be the young person's guiding spirit throughout life. This spirit might point to a warrior's path, or indicate a life as a shaman (medicine man). After receiving the vision, the young person returned to the tribe with a new path to follow. A medicine bundle was made to hold sacred objects associated with the vision. These objects were used throughout life to call on the spirit for help and guidance.

Young men joined warrior societies and lived in their own lodges until marriage. They were responsible for hunting for the tribe. Before going into battle or out to hunt, the warriors decorated themselves with paint. They carried special shields made from the thick shoulder hide of the buffalo, each decorated with powerful personal signs. They performed rituals and dances to ask for courage and success.

Killing an enemy might be an act of great courage, but even more bold was to count coup: a

Medicine bundle

warrior would race up to a foe and strike him with his hand or with a long coup stick decorated with feathers. It showed great bravery to get close enough to strike an enemy in this way. The warriors made prisoners of the women and children of their enemies, often absorbing them into their own tribe.

The great events of the year—from a child's birth to the death of a great chief, from the first green grasses to the winter snows—were recorded on "winter counts," histories painted on tanned buffalo hides. Symbols of events such as meteor showers, great battles, or especially abundant herds showed the highlights of the past year.

When they visited the Yankton Sioux camp, the captains and their men sat around fires at the center of what Clark described as "a village consisting of about 40 handsome, cone-shaped lodges covered with red and white painted buffalo and elk skins." This was the first time Clark had seen tipis. The Sioux lived in these dwellings made of tall poles and animal skins. The smoke from a fire in the center of the tipi traveled up and out of a hole left in the top. Tipis were decorated with geometrical patterns or paintings of animals or warriors' brave deeds.

Families of 12 to 15 people—parents and children, grandparents, unmarried uncles and aunts—lived in each of the large tipis. When it was time to move, the women of the tribe broke the tipis down and loaded them on to poles called travois, which were dragged by horses and dogs. In no time, the band was moving across the grass-covered plains. The men rode on horseback in front and on both sides of the traveling tribe. The children perched on top of the bundles on the travois, and their mothers walked beside them. Their dogs trotted along behind.

means "Campers at the End of the Circle."

The Minneconjou, whose name means "Planters Beside the Water."

The Oglala, who got their name from the word for throwing something at a person.

The Itazipco, whose name in French was *Sans Arc*, meaning "Without Bows."

The Oohenonpa, called Two Kettles.

"Sioux" was the name Lewis and Clark used, a shortened French version of "Nadowesiu." This name came from the Ojibwa, who fought against the Sioux, and it means "Little Snake" or "Enemy." The Santee Sioux are the Dakota nation, the Yankton Sioux are the Nakota nation, and the Teton Sioux are the Lakota nation.

A Winter Count

You can tell the story of your year in pictographs (pictures representing ideas), as the Sioux did on their winter counts.

Materials

- *Large brown paper bag*
- *Pencil*
- *Scissors*
- *Paints and brushes or markers or crayons*

Trace an outline on the bag in the shape of a hide, like the one in the illustration, then cut it out. Paint or draw 12 pictures on the hide, each representing an event that happened during one month of your year. Important events depicted on some winter counts were meteor showers (shown by a star with a long trailing tail), visions or great medicine (pictures of people's heads connected to images of their spirit guides above them), and the capture of many horses (lots of hoofprints). Perhaps your family moved one month—you could draw or paint a picture of a travois (or the modern-day version, a moving van). Did you make a new friend? You could show that by drawing two people shaking hands. Make your own personalized winter count or make one for a friend or family member as a way to celebrate a birthday.

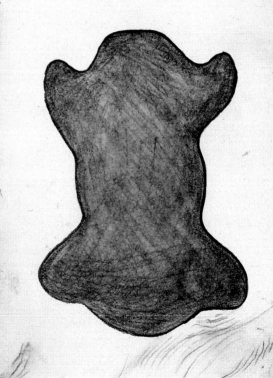

Make a Tipi

Plains Indians traveled far to forested lands to get poles for their tipis, or they traded valuable goods to obtain them from other tribes. For each tipi, they killed and skinned more than a dozen buffalo, soaked the hides in a mixture of ash and water, scraped off the hair, and scoured the hides with the brains of the buffalo. With a sharpened bone, they worked over the hide for hours, then they smoked it to make it soft and supple. Here's an easier way.

Materials

- *3 yards of 60-inch muslin or other heavy cotton fabric*
- *A 60-inch piece of string*
- *Pencil or marker*
- *Scissors*
- *Measuring tape*
- *Pins*
- *Thread*
- *Sewing machine*
- *7 bamboo poles, 6 feet long and approximately ¼ inch in diameter*
- *Optional: acrylic paints and brushes or markers*

Adult help suggested.

1. Lay fabric out flat. Roll the 60-inch piece of string along one long side of the fabric, and when you reach the end of the string, mark the spot (we'll call that spot the center point). Have another person hold that end of the string at the center point. Attach a pencil or marker to the other end of the string and mark off an arc from one end of the fabric all the way around until you go off the edge of the fabric (see drawing). Draw a straight line from the place where you went off the edge to the center point.
2. Cut along the arc and the straight line.

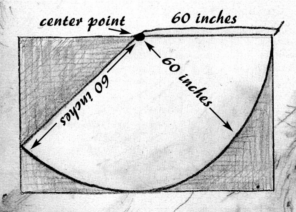

center point   60 inches

60 inches

60 inches

33

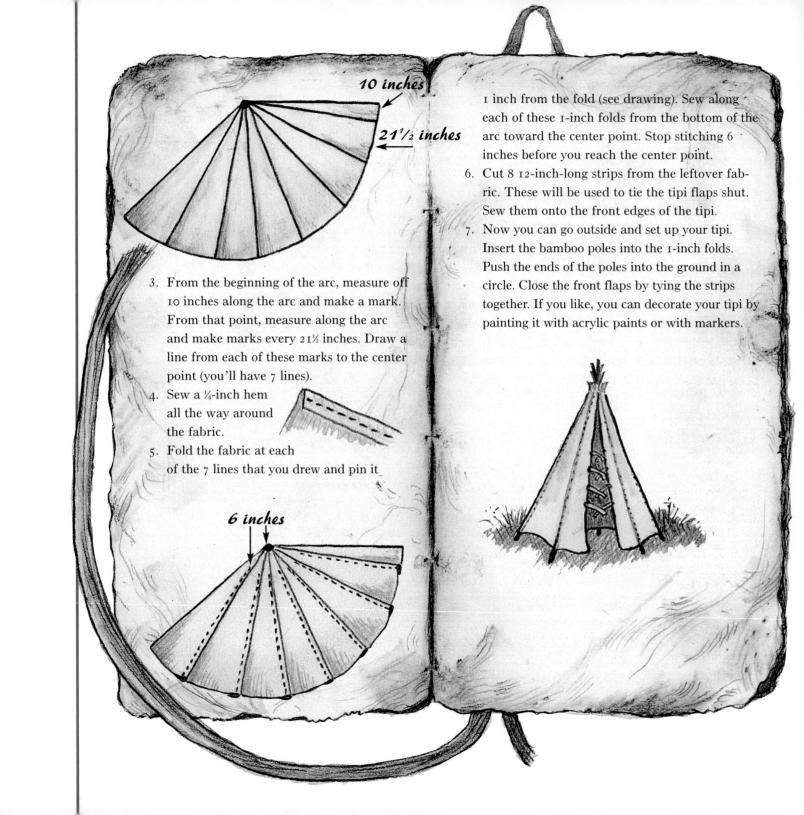

10 inches

21½ inches

3. From the beginning of the arc, measure off 10 inches along the arc and make a mark. From that point, measure along the arc and make marks every 21½ inches. Draw a line from each of these marks to the center point (you'll have 7 lines).

4. Sew a ¼-inch hem all the way around the fabric.

5. Fold the fabric at each of the 7 lines that you drew and pin it

6 inches

1 inch from the fold (see drawing). Sew along each of these 1-inch folds from the bottom of the arc toward the center point. Stop stitching 6 inches before you reach the center point.

6. Cut 8 12-inch-long strips from the leftover fabric. These will be used to tie the tipi flaps shut. Sew them onto the front edges of the tipi.

7. Now you can go outside and set up your tipi. Insert the bamboo poles into the 1-inch folds. Push the ends of the poles into the ground in a circle. Close the front flaps by tying the strips together. If you like, you can decorate your tipi by painting it with acrylic paints or with markers.

The Sioux broke camp often, for they followed the migrating buffalo herds. The men hunted them on horseback. They closed in on the herd at a gallop to separate one animal from the group before shooting it at close range with bows and arrows. After a successful hunt, the tribe held a great feast. Any meat left over was cut into strips and dried, then stored for the months when no buffalo were to be found. When pounded with fat and chokecherries, the dried meat was called pemmican. Girls and women spent hours working over the buffalo skins with sharpened bones, scraping the skins clean. They then treated the skins to soften them and made them into tipis, leggings, shirts, and dresses.

Clark described the Sioux as bold-looking people, handsome and strong. The dancing warriors were decorated with paint. They wore breechcloths and leggings, and feathers and quills in their hair. (An eagle feather in a warrior's hair was significant, an indication that the man had killed an enemy in battle.) Some wore breastplates made of bones and feathers. As the drums beat and the rattles shook in the Sioux village at night, the men stamped and shouted and thrust their weapons high in the air.

A Dance Rattle

ative Americans didn't shop for supplies at grocery stores, craft shops, or hardware stores. They made weapons and tools from things they found in nature. See if you can make this rattle from items found around the house.

Materials

- Construction paper
- Scissors
- Empty baking-powder can with plastic lid
- Glue
- Skewer (or something else that can make a small hole in a plastic lid)
- One chopstick
- A small handful of dried beans or whole black peppercorns
- Markers or paints
- 3 feet of yarn or embroidery thread in 2 or 3 different colors
- Feathers

1. Cut a piece of construction paper so that it fits around the baking-powder can. Use markers or paints to decorate it with your own design, then glue it onto the can.

2. Use the skewer to carefully make a small hole in the center of the lid. Place the lid back on the can. Push the chopstick through the hole all the way to the bottom of the can, then make a mark on it where it goes through the lid. Remove the chopstick.

3. Glue feathers to the top end of the chopstick. Wind strands of yarn or embroidery thread around it from the top to just below the mark (see drawing). Tie off the yarn with a knot.

4. Place beans or peppercorns in the can. Push the chopstick through the lid, then place a big drop of glue on its

bottom end. Put the lid on the can, and push the chopstick firmly against the bottom. Let dry for an hour.

5. Cut out four pieces of colored construction paper, 2½ inches by 3 inches. Cut each piece into very thin strips, leaving a ¼-inch margin at one end (see drawing). Place glue on each ¼-margin and stick these pieces around the lid. Cut a circle out of another piece of colored paper and glue it to the bottom of the dance rattle.

What Causes Extinction?

Scientists estimate that as many as 100 species on our planet become extinct every day! There are more than 200 endangered animal species in the United States, including some of the animals described by Lewis and Clark.

There are natural causes for extinction, such as climate change, but more often species become extinct because of human interference. Sometimes they are hunted to extinction, as the buffalo nearly was. Most of the time, extinction is caused by something you may not even think about—habitat degradation. This means that the habitat, or living environment of a species, is taken over or changed in such a way that the species can no longer feed or shelter its population. Habitat degradation happens when people build dams or clear-cut forests, or when other animals are introduced to an area and take over the food supply. The pronghorn, for instance, needs wide open grassland to thrive. When settlers moved west, their cattle took over the grassland. Ranchers placed barbed-wire fences around their land and the pronghorn injured themselves on them—they didn't know how to jump fences. The fences also cut them off from their water supplies. Pronghorn numbers were reduced from more than 50 million to only 15,000. When hunting was controlled and habitat was set aside for them, their numbers increased again, so now there are more than 750,000.

It's important to learn more about the habitat requirements of plants and animals and to think of ways that we can share our planet with them. You can help, too.

- Find out which plants are native to your region. Plant them in your backyard or in a window box.
- Plant flowers for butterflies and bees.
- Build a bird feeder or a birdhouse.
- Volunteer at a local wildlife refuge or nature center.
- Raise money for a nature organization.
- Write to your representative in Congress about your concerns.
- Recycle everything you can think of. Buy less stuff. Choose earth-friendly products—check the labels! Turn off the lights and air conditioning. Use cold water instead of hot. Walk rather than drive. Pick up litter.
- Learn everything you can about an endangered species and start a group at school to help save it.

The Prairie Dog

The prairie dog isn't a dog at all. It's a rodent, most closely related to the squirrel and the chipmunk. Prairie dogs are found only in the open, grassy plains of North America. Generally around one foot long (not including a short tail), they have tan-colored fur that blends in with the brown grasses of its habitat. Prairie dogs have short legs, tiny ears, beady brown eyes, and cheek pouches. They eat grasses, weeds, roots, and leaves. They're social animals who live in family groups called "coteries." The coteries gather in large "towns" of hundreds or even thousands. (One such town in Texas had 400 million prairie dog citizens!) They dig elaborate underground burrows 10- to 15-feet deep with side tunnels and chambers. During the day, prairie dogs like to stand on the mounds looking about. If they see danger (hawks, coyotes, and ferrets prey on prairie dogs), they squeak loudly to warn everyone in the town, then quickly dive underground.

September 7, 1804
The men hunt for prairie dog

The expedition set out from the village early the next day. Dorion stayed behind with the Sioux. The journey took the men past buffalo, elk, and deer. Wolf packs followed the herds.

The expedition also met an entirely new animal. It looked like a squirrel but without the squirrel's big bushy tail, and it lived underground. As the captains were walking one day, they saw hundreds of these creatures standing on mounds in the short grass. The animals disappeared into holes instantly when the men approached, then their little heads popped up again when they felt that danger was past. They barked like dogs, which inspired their name—prairie dogs.

Lewis wanted one of the little animals to send back to President Jefferson. The men spent hours trying to catch one! Whenever a prairie dog emerged from a hole, everyone raced and dove to catch it. The little creatures were too quick for them and ducked back to safety every time. Next, the men tried digging into their tunnels, but after hours of shoveling they realized that they would never catch a prairie dog that way—the tunnels were far too deep. Finally they forced one out by pouring water into its tunnel; they surrounded and caught it when it emerged, soaking wet.

The men saw their first mule deer on this part of the journey. This animal, with its large ears and black-tipped tail, was also new to them. Another long-eared creature that caught their attention was a white-tailed jackrabbit. The rabbit astonished Lewis, who measured its tracks. Its leaps were 21 feet long! The men saw another animal that looked somewhat like a goat and somewhat like an antelope. It was neither. The animal they had discovered was a creature that is found only on the North American plains—the pronghorn. The fastest animal in North America, the pronghorn seemed to fly across the ground when danger approached (they can run up to 70 miles an hour). When they were frightened, the white hair on their rumps raised up as a warning signal to the other animals. With black masks and horns, tan coats with white bellies, and two white bands crossing their throats, the pronghorns looked unlike any other animal Lewis and Clark had ever seen. They were, too, for the pronghorn is not closely related to any other animal in the world.

One day the men found signs of an animal that had lived on the plains long ago. They had discovered a fossil backbone, 45 feet long, on an island in the river.

On another day, when he was walking through the grasses, Lewis flushed out a plump, tan-colored bird with a long tail—a sharp-tailed grouse. He also discovered a black-billed magpie with a "remarkable long tale."

The captains and their men couldn't get over the abundance of this land. Every day was a new miracle. In every direction, Lewis wrote, they saw "Vast herds of Buffaloe deer Elk and Antilopes feeding . . . as far as the eye of the observer could reach." Mice, gophers, and rabbits made their homes in the prairie grasses, as did birds like the meadowlark, the killdeer, and the plover. Hawks circled overhead looking for prey. The prairie was the home of the giant whooping crane, big as a human being. Ducks paddled along the river or in potholes on the prairie. As the sun set and the men made camp, other animals made their presence felt. Hooting owls, howling wolves, and croaking frogs competed with the sounds of Cruzatte's fiddle.

Lewis gathered plants, many of them new to science. He couldn't wait to send them to Jefferson. The president would be very pleased to receive these samples, for he was a passionate gardener and botanist. Clark must have been especially impressed by one plant that seemed to be everywhere—the prickly pear—for he named a creek after it. He named other creeks for members of the expedition. And perhaps he was hungry the day he named Biscuit Creek!

One day the expedition rounded a bend in the river, and the men saw a sight that made them glad. Their long-lost companion, George Shannon, was sitting on the bank. The boy had followed the river, hoping that at some point the expedition's boats would pass by. They happened on him just in time, for he hadn't eaten in many days. Though there were animals everywhere, he had run out of ammunition and wasn't able to hunt. One of the horses had disappeared. Shannon had been living on berries he had found along the river. Thin and weak, he clambered aboard the keelboat, grateful to be reunited with his comrades.

Shannon was safe, but the whole expedition was endangered a short time later. Captain Clark awoke with a start one night, not quite sure what had awakened him. He then saw by the light of the moon that the sandbar island they had camped on was giving way to the rushing currents of the Missouri River. Chunks of land crashed and fell into the swift water. Soon the whole island would sink with the men and their supplies! Clark roused everyone, and the men quickly boarded the boats and pushed off from the bank. By the time they got on the river, the island they'd been sleeping on only moments before had crashed into the water and disintegrated.

September 25, 1804
The expedition encounters the Teton Sioux

Two nights later, as the expedition camped along the river, three young Indian boys swam across from the opposite bank. George Drouillard, who knew how to use the Indian sign language, learned from them that people of their tribe, the Teton Sioux, were camped close by. The captains gave the boys tobacco and a message for their chiefs—they would like to hold council with them.

As the expedition paddled upriver toward the Teton

White Buffalo Calf Woman

The Sioux people received the first pipe from White Buffalo Calf Woman. During a great famine, White Buffalo Calf Woman came to the people dressed in shining white buckskin and carrying a bundle of sage leaves. "I am bringing something holy," she said, "a message for the people from the buffalo nation." She sang to them, and a white, sweet-smelling cloud

came out of her mouth. She unwrapped the bundle and showed the people a sacred pipe. She taught them to lift the pipe up to the sky and to lower it down to the earth and told them that by holding the pipe, they formed a bridge between the sacred sky and the sacred earth. She taught them that the people were one with all living things. After promising to return, White Buffalo Calf Woman walked into the setting sun. As she walked away, she stopped and rolled over four times, each time taking a different form. She became a black buffalo, then a brown buffalo,

Sioux camp the next day, Private John Colter rode along the bank hunting. He came running back to the river on foot, shouting to his comrades that Indians had taken his horse. Shortly after the captains heard this news, they saw five Indians on the bank of the river. They had Drouillard sign to them that they wanted the horse returned, and that they were not afraid of the Indians. Still, the incident must have put the expedition on their guard, for when they got close to the Sioux village, the men anchored the keelboat offshore and placed extra sentries on duty for the night.

Once again, the expedition prepared for a council, pulling gifts out of its stores, raising the flag, and setting up the awning. This time, a large group came to hear Lewis's speech—three chiefs and 30 tall and muscular warriors. The Indians brought gifts of buffalo meat. Drouillard's sign language couldn't keep up with the speech. The captain eventually gave up, showed off his air gun, and handed out gifts. He gave the special peace medals to the chiefs. Two of the chiefs, The Partisan and Buffalo Medicine, weren't impressed with the speech or the gifts. The captains, hoping to soothe them, gave them a tour of the keelboat and a drink.

When they tried to bring the chiefs ashore, The Partisan wouldn't leave. He threatened the captains, saying he would not let the expedition move on until he received more gifts. Three of his warriors grabbed the boat's rope and refused to let it go. Another warrior got on board and wrapped himself around the mast. More words were exchanged.

The Partisan said the Indians would destroy them if the Corps tried to go any farther. Clark replied that his men, too, were warriors, ready to

fight. The Partisan drew his sword. Lewis ordered the men to have their weapons ready. They loaded the large gun on the bow of their keelboat and pointed it at the Indians. The warriors along the shore took arrows from their quivers and held their bows ready. It was a tense moment, and the captains were prepared to give the order to fight.

Just then, the third chief, Black Buffalo, stepped in. He took the rope from the warriors and told the man hugging the mast to get off the boat. Lewis and Clark ordered their men to get ready to row upriver. Clark, hoping to smooth things over, approached The Partisan and Buffalo Medicine and offered to shake hands. They refused his gesture, and Clark left them and boarded his boat. The expedition was just about to leave when Black Buffalo and two of his warriors waded out into the water. Black Buffalo asked if they could join the expedition for the night. The captains said yes and Black Buffalo and the warriors got on board.

They tied the boats up on an island that night and kept a wary guard. Just the day before, Clark had named an island in the river "Good-Humored Island" because it had been a full and lucky day. But, he named the island they camped on that night "Bad-Humored Island." The encounter with the Teton Sioux had left him in a bad temper.

The next day the expedition traveled to Black Buffalo's village as hundreds of Indians watched from the banks of the river. Some of the Sioux men had hawk feathers in their hair. They wore buffalo robes and moccasins with animal pelts tied to the heels.

When the boats reached Black Buffalo's village, the chief invited the captains to stay with his people. He showed them the greatest honors. He had them carried into the village on white buffalo robes and set down in the council house, a large tipi that held 70 men. There the captains smoked the pipe of peace with the chief.

The pipe ritual was a very important part of Sioux culture. People would smoke the pipe while sitting in a circle that represented the Great Spirit, Wakan Tanka. (The universe of the Sioux—the sun, moon, stars, and the earth and its creatures—was thought of as circles within circles, a sacred hoop. When tribes set up their camps, they placed their tipis in a circle to symbolize this belief.)

Black Buffalo pointed the pipe to the sky and the earth, and in the four directions. He lit the pipe, then presented it to the captains to smoke. The Indians made gifts of buffalo meat to the captains. They shared a meal, then watched as the women of the band danced around a large fire. The Teton Sioux had recently won a great victory over an enemy band of Omaha, and as the women danced, they raised the scalps taken as trophies of the battle. Musicians played drums and rattled long sticks with the hooves of deer and elk tied to them. The music and dancing went on late into the night until the tired captains ordered their men back on board the boats to sleep. Captain Clark wrote about this day in his journal, noting the painted faces of the dancing women and the meal of pemmican, dog, and ground potato (actually a root known as the prairie turnip). Even with his worries about the intentions of the Teton Sioux band, he was interested in everything he saw.

When the men of the expedition woke, their boats were surrounded by a crowd of curious onlook-

then a red one. The fourth time, she became a white buffalo calf. Ever since that time, the Sioux have honored the beings with whom they share the earth, and the Great Spirit, Wakan Tanka, with the sacred pipe ceremony.

On the Contrary

If Clark had been a Sioux Heyoka, he would have reversed the names of the islands. The Heyoka, or Contrary, was the sacred clown of the Sioux tribes. He did everything backward! He said yes when he meant no. When it was cold, he wiped his brow and pretended it was very hot. He sat backward on his horse and walked on his hands. By showing things in reverse, the Heyoka was trying to teach the members of his community. For instance, if the Heyoka put his hand in the fire, young children knew that it meant they shouldn't. By doing the opposite, the Heyoka taught what was customary. The Heyoka represented a spirit and was considered a visionary.

Sioux children and those of other Plains tribes were sometimes given a birth name that described their appearance, then later given another name. They were named after their grandparents or for brave deeds or good qualities of their parents. A girl kept her birth name for life, unless she happened to become gravely ill or undergo a crisis of some kind. Then she would receive a new, hopefully luckier, name. A boy received a new name when he became a man (after becoming a successful hunter or after receiving a vision). This new name reflected his actions or was a name inspired by his guardian spirit.

ers. The captains spent another day in the Teton Sioux village. Clark noted that some of the people had run arrows through their flesh above and below their elbows. It was a symbol of grief for a loved one who had died. That night there was once again a spirited dance around a roaring fire. The women raised poles topped with the scalps of their enemies and danced with spears held over their heads.

Some Omaha prisoners were being held in the Sioux village. Pierre Cruzatte spoke the Omaha language, and he visited with the prisoners. They told him that the Teton Sioux had bad intentions and would not let the expedition proceed upriver. Cruzatte repeated the tale to his captains. It might not have been true, but it made them uneasy.

When they returned to the boats that night, an accident made the jumpy captains even more nervous. The Partisan and another warrior had walked with the captains from the village to the river. Clark got in one of the pirogues to row out to the keelboat, which was tied in the middle of the river. In the dark, the pirogue collided with the keelboat's anchor line and snapped it. The keelboat started to tip. Clark shouted out to the men on board to take to the oars and right the boat. The Partisan, who didn't know what Clark was shouting about, thought the white men were about to attack. He began to shout too, and soon Black Buffalo and 200 warriors appeared, ready for battle. It was another tense moment, but everyone soon realized that there was no reason to fight.

The captains decided to leave the next day, anxious to be on their way before another incident occurred. As they prepared to move on, Black Buffalo boarded their boat and asked them to remain another day. Several of his warriors grabbed the boat's cable and appeared to be holding the boat hostage. Was this it? Would the Sioux stop them from proceeding on their journey? Clark spoke sharply, demanding that they let go of the rope. Black Buffalo once again stepped in. He insisted that the captains give the warriors tobacco as a token of respect to the Sioux. Clark threw some tobacco over to the shore. Black Buffalo left the boat and took the rope away from his warriors. The expedition was free to go.

For days they made steady progress. The men saw several small groups of Teton Sioux traveling along the river but managed to stay clear of them and out of trouble. It was now October, and the days were growing shorter and the weather colder. As the expedition moved north, flocks of migrating birds passed overhead on their way south. Ducks and geese in huge numbers flew in v-shaped patterns across the sky. Swans flapped their great wings and flew south. It was comforting to edge close to the fire at night.

October 8–12, 1804
The expedition stays with the Arikara

One day the expedition came upon an Indian village on an island in the river. Men, women, and children rushed from their lodges to watch as the keelboat and pirogues approached. The men landed the boats on the bank of the river to make camp, and Lewis and several men paddled a pirogue over to the village.

The village was a busy settlement of Arikara, one of three villages along this part of the Missouri

River. Lewis found two Frenchmen living among them. They spoke the Arikara language and knew much about their ways. Lewis learned that the Arikara were an agricultural tribe that grew beans, corn, sunflowers, squash, and tobacco in the large gardens around their lodges. They traded with the Sioux and other tribes. They didn't live in tipis like the Sioux, but instead built huge round lodges of poles, willow branches, and grass and covered them with clay. Wood for building was hard to find in the mostly treeless land. The Arikara obtained the wood during spring floods, when huge trees came crashing down the Missouri River. Large families lived inside the lodges along with their dogs and horses. (Horses were cherished by the tribe; inside they were safe from enemies and winter's cold.) The people also cached, or stored, their winter's supply of food in their lodges. Large holes were dug in the dirt floors, filled with corn, and covered back up.

The expedition stayed for five days with the Arikara. Clark thought highly of these generous people. The men, he noted, were tall and well-built. He also noticed the women, who were busy harvesting their crops. They used hoes made from the buffalo's shoulder bone and rakes made from deer antlers. They also gathered wood and prepared the meals. Clark was especially impressed when he saw three women in a bullboat, a special round boat made of willow branches and buffalo hide, coming down the Missouri River on a particularly rough day. The waves were higher than Clark had ever seen them, but the women managed their little boat with ease in the rough currents.

Arikara from the other two villages came to the men's camp to visit and satisfy their curiosity about the strangers. They were especially curious about York, for though white fur traders had visited their villages, they had never seen a black man. York thoroughly enjoyed the attention. He was constantly in the center of a crowd. He showed his muscles and pretended to be a fierce monster. He said he ate young children. Clark worried that he would frighten the Indians by making himself appear to be so terrible.

The men had enjoyed their visit but it was time to move on. The year was coming to a close. Winter was coming and the expedition would have to stop to make a winter camp. In their council with

York with the Arikara

Great Plains Stew

The Arikara raised corn, beans, and squash. Here's a recipe you can make that uses all three. (We left out the buffalo!)

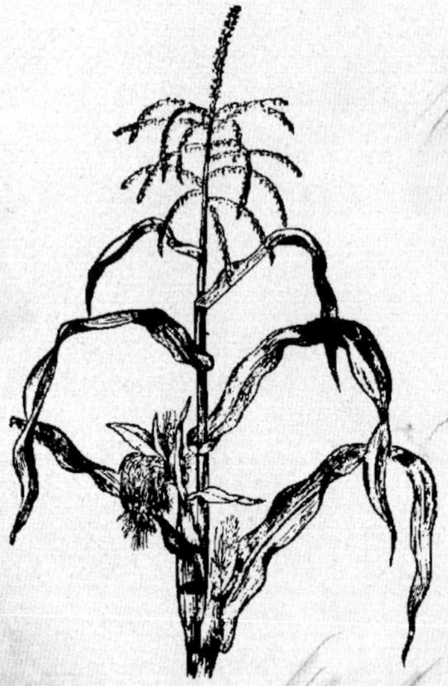

Materials

- Large saucepan
- Wooden spoon
- 2 tablespoons butter
- 3 green onions, thinly sliced
- ½ acorn or butternut squash, peeled and cut into 1-inch chunks
- 1 cup fresh (two ears) or frozen corn kernels
- 1 cup canned white beans
- ¼ teaspoon thyme
- ½ cup milk
- ½ cup water
- 1 square vegetable bouillon

Adult help suggested.

Cook green onions and squash in butter in a large saucepan for five minutes over medium heat. Stir in corn and beans. Add thyme. Add milk, water, and bouillon. Heat, stirring, until mixture boils. Turn heat down to low, and simmer for 15 minutes. Season with salt and pepper, then ladle into bowls and serve.

the Arikara chiefs, Lewis and Clark gave them gifts of vermilion dye, beads, mirrors, knives, tomahawks, sugar and salt. The chiefs thanked them and told them their road was open before them. They gave food to the captains—corn, bread, and special beans that the Indian women gathered from the stores of the meadow mouse. The delicious beans were a favorite of the Arikara. The women gathered them eagerly, but not wanting to deprive the little mice of their meal, they always replaced the beans in the mice's hiding place with corn or other food.

Lewis gathered samples of the Indian corn, beans, and tobacco to save for President Jefferson. The men packed the boats and set off again. One of the Arikara chiefs, Is a Whippoorwill, joined them for the next stage of their journey. He wished to make peace with the tribe that lived upriver—the Mandan.

Lewis and Clark learned one more thing about the Arikara from Is a Whippoorwill. The chief watched as the Corps held a trial for one of the men. The private was charged with mutiny, for he had spoken out against the captains in a threatening way. Ten of the men served as the jury, and they found the private guilty. His punishment was a lashing. The chief was alarmed and cried out when he saw the private being whipped. He told Lewis and Clark that his nation never treated any of its people in that way. They didn't even spank their children when they were naughty. In most Plains tribes, if children did something wrong, they were simply asked to stop. Sometimes mischievous children were splashed with water.

The weather was growing colder. In the mornings the ground was frosted, and ice began to form along the edges of the river. One day it snowed. The Corps wouldn't be able to travel along the river for much longer before the winter's freeze. In the distance, on the western horizon, the men saw ranges of hills. Again there were great herds of buffalo. Deer and elk were abundant. One day they saw a river otter. They also saw the tracks of a bear, huge tracks that Clark described as three times as large as a man's. He wrote, too, about the wolves who followed the herds of buffalo. "When the buffalow move those animals follow, and feed on those that are killed by accident or those that are too pore or fat to keep up."

One day the expedition met a band of Mandan, who were out hunting for food for their village. The captains stopped to greet them and smoked a pipe with their chief, Big White. The Mandan lived in villages nearby, side by side with two villages of the Hidatsa tribe (Lewis and Clark referred to this tribe as the Minnetarees). The people were friendly and welcoming, and the captains decided to make winter camp near their villages. The expedition continued upriver. One cold day late in October, it reached the first village of the Mandan. The expedition's journey was over for the year.

An Arikara Story

As the boats moved upriver, they passed several large stones in the open prairie. According to Arikara legend, one of them had once been a man, the other a young woman. They were in love, but their parents would not allow them to marry. The man walked off into the plains to mourn, and the young woman followed him. Her dog followed at her heels. As they walked, they gathered grapes to eat. Slowly, from their feet to their heads, all three turned to stone. The grapes that the woman held turned to stone, too. Clark retold the story in his journal and also noted that the Arikara "pay reverence" to those stones and that there was a large quantity of grapes growing near them.

The Wolf

The intelligent and adaptable wolf is one of nature's best hunters. Wolves hunt big animals such as deer, elk, and buffalo, and small animals like squirrels, rabbits, and birds. They even hunt fish! Wolves adapt their hunting style to the animal they're stalking and the ground they're covering. A lone wolf will pounce on mice in a field. To catch larger prey, wolves hunt in a cooperative pack. They separate an animal from the herd and run it down until it's too exhausted to fight. As Clark observed, they most often prey on those animals weakened in some way—those that are old, young, or sick. More often than not, the wolves fail at their attempts to catch their prey. Sometimes a wolf gives chase to an animal just to see how strong the animal is. If it looks like it will put up a fight, the wolf gives up right away. Wolf packs were a common sight around the edges of the buffalo herds. Unless the wolves were actively hunting, the buffalo paid little attention to them.

Wolves can detect smells from miles away. Their hearing and eyesight are excellent. Wolves can even read other animals' tracks. They are such great hunters that the Indians adopted some of their ways. For instance, wolves know that pronghorns are curious animals. If a pronghorn sees a moving object and doesn't sense danger, it will approach to investigate. Wolves hunt pronghorn by lying in the grass and wagging their tails in the air to attract them. Indians hunted pronghorn in the same way, hiding in the grass and waving a stick in the air to bring them closer.

Even though wolves are such excellent hunters, sometimes they must go for days without a meal. When wolves catch their prey, they gorge until they are full, then take a long nap. If it's spring and there are cubs in the den, the adult wolves swallow some meat and bring it to the den, where they regurgitate (throw up) the partially digested food for the hungry pups.

4

Forty-Five Below

October 25, 1804
The expedition reaches the Mandan and Hidatsa villages and searches for a site for its winter fort

Within a few days, the expedition had visited each of five villages along the river. About 4,000 people of the Mandan and Hidatsa tribes lived in the cluster of villages. It seemed as if most of them flocked to see the white men's boats! Lewis and Clark held councils with the chiefs of the villages, helped once again by a French fur trader who made his home there. The Mandan and Hidatsa chiefs welcomed the expedition and the Arikara chief, Is a Whippoorwill, and together they smoked the pipe of peace. Each of the Mandan and Hidatsa chiefs was given one of President Jefferson's peace medals, a flag, a coat, and a hat. The Indians gave gifts of corn and meat to the captains. Black Cat, a great chief of the Mandan, walked with the captains along the river to help them pick a site for a winter camp. Clark gave a glazed earthen jar to Black Cat's wife in return. She accepted it "with much pleasure."

The Corps of Discovery entering a Mandan Village

Replica of Fort Mandan

The first few days were busy with back-and-forth visiting and councils. One night, one of the chiefs brought his small sons to the expedition's camp to watch the men dance to Cruzatte's fiddle. Some of the French voyagers who had paddled upstream with the expedition built a boat and headed back down the Missouri River to St. Louis before winter set in. Arikara Chief Is a Whippoorwill went back home accompanied by several Mandan who wished to establish a peace.

One day the men witnessed a huge prairie fire. Fires were common in the grassy lands. Sometimes lightning started the fires, but they often were set on purpose by the Indians to send messages to faraway tribes or to burn off dry grass and let new green grass grow to attract buffalo. In this fire, two people died. One boy was saved by his quick-thinking mother, who threw a fresh buffalo skin over him. The fire burned a circle around the boy but did not penetrate the buffalo skin.

The captains chose a site for their camp on the east bank of the river and set the men to work building a fort. They made eight rough log cabins of cottonwood trees, built in two rows that met at an angle. They filled the cracks in the logs with mud to keep out the chilly wind. They built two large storage rooms and an 18-foot tall protective fence. They fashioned desks, beds, tables, and benches out of cottonwood trees. Lastly, they built stone fireplaces. They finished their fort three weeks later and named it Fort Mandan. That night, seven inches of snow fell.

Fort Mandan was a busy place that winter. Every day the men performed drills, cleaned their weapons, and took turns standing guard. On the most frigid days, they changed the guard every half hour so no one got too cold. The men drew their water from the river. Sometimes they had to chop through the ice to reach it! Drouillard, the best hunter, took parties out to hunt for food. One day, Mandan hunters invited the men along on their buffalo hunt. They were amazed at the skill of the Indians riding bareback on their ponies. The Indians guided the swift horses with their knees as they herded the stampeding buffalo.

As winter progressed, the hunters had to go farther afield to find game. They tramped for miles tracking animals. Some days the snow and bright sun blinded them. Other days gray sky blended into the horizon and it was hard to tell which way to turn. Some of the men got frostbite from the icy wind and low temperatures. Once, Lewis was still far from the fort when night fell. He spent the night sleeping in the cold under the hide of a buffalo he had killed.

When the men were not hunting or standing guard, they repaired equipment for the next stage of

The Legend of the Lost Welshmen

Many people once believed that a lost colony of ancient voyagers could be found among the Indians of the west. There is a legend that 10 ships led by a prince of Wales named Madoc had sailed across the Atlantic Ocean in 1170 and then sailed up the mouth of the Mississippi River, never to be seen again. Some thought the Welshmen had settled with Indians and that their descendants still lived somewhere in the west.

Thomas Jefferson instructed Meriwether Lewis to look for signs of the long-lost voyagers. Some visitors to the Mandan villages thought the Mandan were the descendants of the Welshmen. "Mandan" and "Madoc" sounded very much alike and among the Mandan were individuals with hazel eyes and light skin. One visitor noticed that the round bullboats used by the tribes in this region were unlike any boats made by other tribes but were very similar to a Welsh boat called a "coracle." Lewis was also struck by the similarity between the stories of a great flood in the Mandan and Christian traditions. However, the legend of the lost Welshmen is now believed to be just that—a legend.

Front feet

Hind feet

Raccoon

Pigeon

Canada goose

Hind feet

Front feet

Cottontail rabbit

Tracking Animals

Tracking was important to the Indians and to the hunters of the expedition, and it was also important to Lewis and Clark for scientific purposes. You can learn a lot about an animal by studying its tracks. You can collect these track prints by making plaster casts of them. Explore nature and see what you can find.

Materials

- Notebook
- Pencil
- Measuring tape or ruler
- Dry plaster of paris
- Jar with a tight lid
- Clean tin can
- Water
- Old spoon or wooden stick
- Plastic knife
- Newspaper
- Old toothbrush

You can find animal tracks in forests and in vacant city lots. Look carefully in the dirt of your backyard or look anywhere after a fresh snowfall.

Each animal's track is different, and in many cases there is even a difference between the front and back feet of a single animal. Sometimes the tracks will differ depending on whether the animal is walking or running. When you find a track, sit down and examine it for a while. Look at the size, the shape, and the number of toes.

Cat and dog tracks are very common and look similar. Size might be one clue in telling the difference, but if the tracks are small look for claw marks to identify the animal. Dogs leave claw marks; cats retract their claws when they walk. Another difference—the dog's front feet touch the ground at a different place from where its hind feet stepped. The cat's hind feet generally step on the same spot its front feet stepped on.

Deer leave tracks that look like two big teardrops.

The raccoon's front feet look like tiny hands; its back feet like little human feet with long toes.

Rabbits hop—they push off the ground with their back legs, and they land in such a way that their hind-feet are in front of their forefeet. You'll see little round pawprints behind the prints of the longer hind feet.

Squirrels have four toes on their front feet and five on their back feet.

If you see tiny tracks with a line between them, you're looking at an animal that has a long tail. A mouse sometimes leaves traces of its tail between footprints.

Opossums also leave tail marks between their unusual prints. Opossum tracks look like a tiny human hand and a tiny human foot with a thumb instead of a big toe. Their feet are made for climbing trees.

Ducks and geese have webbed feet. Some birds (like pigeons) walk by putting one foot in front of the other (as we do). Other birds hop, leaving footprints that are side by side. If you see bird tracks on the snow, look carefully beside them—you might see the barest trace of the wings' feathers in the snow.

Front feet

Hind feet

Opossum

Sometimes you can tell a story from tracks. Where was the animal going, and what was it doing? Was it running away? Was it looking for food? Look for other clues, such as gnawed branches, nests, droppings, claw marks on trees, and piles of acorns.

Keep a scientific record of your tracking adventures. Bring a notebook and pencil and draw the tracks you find. Measure them and write the dimensions in your notebook. Measure the distance between prints, too, so you know the length of the animal's stride or leap. Write down the date and place where you saw the tracks.

Carry dry plaster of paris (in a tightly-closed jar) on your walk. When you see a track you want to save, make plaster. Place two tablespoons of water in the tin can. Add three tablespoons of dry plaster, sifting it through your fingers. Let the mixture rest for a few minutes, then stir. Pour it carefully into the tracks and let it harden for 10 minutes. Cut around the plaster with a knife, then dig beneath it a couple of inches and gently lift it out. Wrap it in newspaper. When you get home, spread the paper out and gently brush the dirt off the plaster cast with a toothbrush.

Cat

Front feet

Dog

Hind feet

Red squirrel

Mule deer

the journey. They made moccasins of deerskin and new shirts and pants to replace their ragged clothing. Lewis served as doctor to his men and to people of the tribes. He treated cuts and frostbite. He drew on the skills his mother had taught him, along with the techniques he'd learned from his teachers in the east. He also paid attention to the ways of the Indians, who treated their sick with special plants and with sweat baths.

Both Lewis and Clark worked diligently on their reports. Lewis noted the weather and the temperature every day. He carefully prepared plant and animal specimens to send back to President Jefferson. Clark worked with the translator and the Indians to make a dictionary of their languages. Late at night both captains sat at their rough cottonwood desks and wrote about their findings by the light of flickering tallow candles. Clark also drew a detailed map of the country. He used his notes from the previous months to help him map out the land they had passed through. He and Lewis spent countless hours with the Mandan and Hidatsa chiefs, questioning them about the land ahead. Clark drew on the Indians' knowledge to map out the country they would venture through when spring came.

Big White and the other chiefs told the captains about the river and about the streams that flowed into it. They told them about the tribes that lived in the lands they would pass through. They told them about the great mountains where the river was born, but beyond that their knowledge faded. Lewis and Clark listened carefully to every detail and asked for more. Big White patiently told them everything he knew. He drew the great river in the dirt floor of his lodge and built tiny moun-

A Hidatsa

tains of sand to show the captains what lay before them.

The captains were especially interested to hear that one tribe that lived near the headwaters of the Missouri River, the Shoshone (or Snake) tribe, was known to have horses. The expedition would need horses to travel over the mountains ahead and find the river that would take them to the ocean. In order to make this journey with all of their supplies, they would need horses. They were counting on buying the horses from the Shoshone.

November 4, 1804
Toussaint Charbonneau and Sacagawea join the expedition

One day a French trader and his Indian wife came to visit the fort. The woman was not of the local tribes, but was a Shoshone from the distant mountains. She had been captured by the Hidatsa when she was 12 and had lived for several years with them on the plains, far from her own people. When the captains discovered that the trader, Toussaint Charbonneau, was married to a woman who spoke the Shoshone language, they hired him for the expedition. They asked Charbonneau to bring his wife, Sacagawea, along to interpret for them when they met the Shoshone. Charbonneau and the young, pregnant Sacagawea set up a tipi inside the fort and joined the expedition.

The winter was bitterly cold. The snow grew deep and icy winds blew. One day the temperature reached 45 degrees below zero! The river froze solid. It was hard to remember the hot summer days when they caught fish in its waters.

People from the Indian villages crossed the frozen river and visited the fort every day. Even in their thin moccasins they didn't seem to mind the cold. They wrapped buffalo robes around their shoulders and came to see the strange men who had traveled to their land. They brought the men pemmican, squash, and beans. The captains, in turn, gave them gifts of fish hooks, beads, ribbons, and mirrors. When they started to run low on the stores of gifts they'd brought from the east, one of the privates came up with an idea to enable them to continue to trade with the tribes. John Shields was a blacksmith and knew how to make and repair iron tools. He set up a forge inside the fort and put it to use repairing broken weapons and making tools for the Indians. A lively trade developed between the villages and the fort.

The men spent time at the Indian villages, too. These tribes were settled; they didn't wander the plains like the Sioux. They lived in earth lodges and raised crops of corn, beans, and squash. They traded these goods with other tribes, such as the Sioux and the Cheyenne, who brought horses, tools, and buffalo hides for exchange. Because trade was so important to the Mandan and Hidatsa, they made a strict rule that no one who came to the villages to trade should be harmed. They hunted the buffalo that came near their villages. A couple of times a

Thick Coats and Long Naps

Some of the animals the men had seen during the summer and fall disappeared during the winter. Others adapted to the cold.

Geese, ducks, cranes, and other birds flew thousands of miles south to spend the winter in a warmer climate. Frogs buried themselves in the mud beneath rivers and breathed in air through their skin. Buffalo grew thick fur and used their massive heads to push the snow off the grass. Wolves herded buffalo onto ice, where they would lose their footing and become easy prey.

Clark was given a weasel that had changed its coat from dark brown to white to blend in with the snow (and avoid becoming someone's dinner)!

Bears "denned up" and took very long naps. Skunks and raccoons slept for weeks at a time. The true hibernators, prairie dogs and ground squirrels, slept underground for months, with body temperatures close to freezing and heart rates just a couple of beats per minute.

year, they went off on extended hunts and lived in tipis like the more nomadic tribes of the Great Plains.

The dome-shaped earth lodges of the Indians housed large families of 20 or more. The lodges were built by digging a large circle two feet deep in the ground and 40 to 60 feet in diameter. Timber poles were placed in the ground all around the edge of the circle. A timber roof was supported by tall beams driven into the dirt floor. A mat of willow boughs covered the roof, then the whole lodge was covered with two to three feet of hard clay. The thick earthen walls kept the lodge warm during the freezing winters and cool during hot summers. Over time the dirt floor became hardened by the scuffling of moccasined feet until it seemed almost polished. Scalps taken by warriors were displayed on poles outside the lodges. Medicine bundles also hung from poles as reminders of sacred powers and spirits.

When the captains visited a chief at his lodge, they stopped at the door and shook a buffalo-hoof rattle to announce their presence. Then they pushed aside a buffalo-skin door to enter. Inside, a fire ring in the center of the lodge provided a warm welcome. Crossed poles over the fire held a large cooking pot. The comforting smells of buffalo stew or prairie turnip pudding combined with the scents of burning sage and sweetgrass. Smoke curled out from a hole in the center of the high roof. Beds around the edges of the lodge were curtained off with painted buffalo skins. Shields and weapons, baskets and tools all had their place in the lodge, as did the dogs and ponies of its occupants.

The lodges were close together, and their doors faced a large open space in the center of the village. In warm weather the women worked the gardens around their lodges, cut wood, and carried water while the men hunted for buffalo, deer, and other game. Large drying racks stood outside each lodge. Drying meat was hung high out of the reach of hungry dogs. Ears of corn were braided together, hung, and stored for the next year's seed. Buffalo skins were stretched for tanning, and the women worked long hours scraping and cleaning them. When their work was done, the people sat on the roofs of their earth lodges, laughing and talking. From the rooftops they could see the whole village, the burial scaffolds outside the ring of lodges, the river, and the wide prairie stretching to the horizon.

In Mandan society the women built and owned the lodges and all the belongings, from tools to horses. These were passed on from mother to daughter, and when a marriage took place the man came to live in the woman's home. Some men had more than one wife; if a man married the oldest daughter of a family he could also marry her sisters. (The French trader Charbonneau, who had lived with the Mandan for many years, had two wives.)

The Indians wore shirts, leggings, and dresses of buckskin, ornamented with porcupine quills and fringe. Moccasins were also beautifully decorated. Quillwork was a sacred craft performed by women of tribes across the plains. They dyed porcupine quills bright colors with dyes made from plants. The women placed the quills in their mouths and drew them out, one at a time, flattening them with their teeth. Then they braided the quills onto pipestems or sewed them onto clothes and moccasins. Thick, warm buffalo robes kept the people warm in the winter. On one side of a robe was the animal's dark hair; on the other side were paintings of battles and great deeds.

The people of the tribes were strong and slender. They painted their faces with vermilion dye.

Buffalo dance of the Mandans

Some of the men painted their hair red. The women parted their hair and braided it, then painted the part with red dye. Warriors placed eagle and raven feathers in their long hair. Some of the chiefs wore elaborate horned headdresses.

Though the Mandan and Hidatsa people were farmers, the hunters and warriors among them held a place of honor. The buffalo was important to them, and they held ceremonies to attract the sacred animal. The Indians believed that the buffalo had a spirit, as did all creatures and objects— rocks and water, the sun and moon, insects, birds, and animals. Their ceremonies, such as the buffalo dance, honored these spirits. The men put buffalo masks on their heads and shouted and danced in a circle while drums beat and onlookers shouted. Hunters pretended to shoot them with arrows, and when they fell, other dancers took their place. The dance continued until buffalo herds appeared near the villages. The women also held a corn dance to ensure a good crop, singing and dancing to the sound of drums and rattles.

The most sacred ceremony was the sun dance. This ceremony was performed by many tribes in the plains. It required months of preparation and purification through praying, fasting, and physical challenges. The ceremony itself lasted for days.

After a successful hunt, the people celebrated their good fortune with a great feast. When the feast was over, they played ball games and held contests. Many bets were placed on horse races, archery contests, and a game in which a lance was thrown through a small ring as it rolled across the ground.

Children learned how to ride horses and to swim at a very young age. In the summer, they

The Mandan and Hidatsa tribes had been living along the upper Missouri River for hundreds of years before the expedition's visit. They came there from the east as part of a great migration. But where did their ancestors come from? Your family may have come to the United States from Europe, Asia, or Africa, or perhaps you have Native American ancestors. Who were these first Americans?

Many scientists believe that the first Americans crossed to the North American continent from Asia approximately 15,000 years ago. At that time the oceans were lower because their waters were captured in the great glaciers of an ice age. When the waters went down, a land bridge was uncovered between Siberia and Alaska. Hunters from Asia crossed the bridge to a new land in pursuit of woolly mammoths and other large game. When the glaciers receded, the lands to the south opened up, and the migrating hunters spread across North and South America. Over time, according to this theory, the hunters divided into different tribes with distinct languages and customs. From the Inuit in the cold north to the Anasazi of the

Hoop and Pole

The hoop and pole game was a favorite in the Mandan and Hidatsa villages. After the children finished playing the game, they would throw their hoops into the Missouri River in the belief that each hoop would turn into a buffalo.

Materials

- *Two teams*
- *Branches for poles, about 3 feet long and ½ inch thick*
- *Thin, flexible branches, about 2 feet long (grapevine wreaths from a craft store or hula hoops can be used instead)*
- *String*

Gather thick branches to use for poles and thin ones to form into hoops. (If you need branches to be cut, get an adult to do this.) Bend each of the thin branches into a circle, then tie them with string so that they stay bent. (Other options for hoops are grapevine wreaths, or to make the game a little easier, hula hoops.) Count your friends off into two teams—a hoop team and a pole team. Give one pole to each member of the pole team.

The pole team lines up along a sidewalk and the members of the hoop team roll their hoops, one at a time, down the sidewalk. The pole team members try to throw their poles through each hoop as it is rolling. A player who gets her pole through a hoop receives one point. When all the hoops have been thrown, switch sides and let the other team try to spear hoops. After you play 10 rounds, the warrior with the most points wins.

In another version of the game, when the hoops are thrown, the pole team tries to catch them with their poles. When a player catches a hoop, he throws it back to the other team. When all the hoops have been caught and thrown back, the players with the poles get to chase the opposing team.

bathed every morning in the river's waters. In the winter their mothers cut holes in the ice and brought water to the lodges or the children washed with snow! Girls played house in miniature lodges made of willow branches and learned how to make and paddle the round bullboats with great skill. They made trampolines from buffalo skins. Boys practiced riding and shooting so they could hunt with their fathers.

In the wintertime the children happily slid down snowbanks on sleds made from the backbone

A Mandan chief

and ribs of a buffalo. They slid buffalo-rib gliders across the ice of the Missouri River in contests to see who could slide the farthest and straightest. They warmed themselves by the lodge fire and listened as their grandparents told stories. The men hunted to feed their families, and the women attended to their many chores.

During this particular winter, however, the Mandan found it much more interesting to visit the white men. They liked the explorers. They called Clark "Red Hair" and Lewis "Long Knife." The large boat of the white men was a curiosity and seemed like great medicine. York, too, seemed like a being of special power.

The captains thought highly of their winter neighbors and were glad to be among people who were so brave and kind. When a group of Mandan hunters was surprised by an attack by enemy warriors, Lewis and Clark offered two dozen strong men and their weapons to their neighbors. Later, a small hunting party from the fort was attacked. Drouillard and three men faced 100 Sioux warriors, who rushed up on them as they were bringing buffalo meat back to the fort. The Indians cut the men's horses from their sleds, and made off with two of the horses. Mandan warriors joined Lewis and a small force as they sought to punish the Sioux for the attack. Bad weather stopped them; the trail was cold. No one could fight, or even walk, through the deep snow that covered the ground.

The men announced Christmas morning with a bang—they fired their guns three times when they raised the flag over the fort. After dinner that night they sang and danced. On New Year's Day, the chiefs of the villages invited the men to celebrate with them. The Indians were greatly pleased by

southwest deserts to the Lakota of the Great Plains, Indian peoples settled across the area that is now the United States.

Not all scientists agree with the land bridge theory. Some believe that the earliest Americans arrived by boat from unknown lands across the Pacific. There is also disagreement about how long ago these ancient people migrated. Estimates vary between 12,000 and 60,000 years ago. Some scientists base their theories on the fact that a tool known as a Clovis point has been uncovered in archeological sites across the Americas. A Clovis point is a stone spearhead with a special groove in its base where it was once attached to a wooden throwing stick. These tools date back to 11,000 years ago. Many scientists date the arrival of early Americans to just before this time.

Other scientists believe that people arrived in the Americas much earlier. A woman's bones found in California were judged to be 13,000 years old. Some tools have been found that seem to predate the Clovis point. Scientists who study genetics compare Native Americans with Asians and calculate a separation occurring between 15,000 and 30,000 years ago. Experts in languages look at the similarities and differences between Native American tribal languages. They calculate the amount of time it would have taken for the first Americans to split up into tribes and develop their own languages. Some of these experts think migrating hunters came here from Asia between 35,000 and 60,000 years ago. Many questions about the first Americans remain unsolved.

Winter village of the Hidatsa

their visitors' antics and Pierre Cruzatte's fiddling. They were especially delighted when Cruzatte danced on his hands for them.

During the cold months the boats became locked in the frozen river. All of the men worked long days trying to pry them out. They hacked at the ice with axes and poured boiling water over it. After weeks of dangerous, exhausting work, they finally freed the pirogues and the keelboat from the icy grip of the Missouri River. They pulled the boats ashore and began repairing them for the spring journey. Lewis and Clark planned to send the keelboat back to St. Louis with the crew of French boatmen. The captains and their chosen men—the Corps of Discovery—would head toward unknown lands up the Missouri River.

February 11, 1805
Sacagawea gives birth to Jean Baptiste "Pomp" Charbonneau

Lewis had treated many cases of frostbite that winter. One day in February his doctoring skills were needed to help Sacagawea give birth. The Indian woman was in great pain; it seemed as if her labor would never end. One of the traders told Lewis of an Indian remedy that would hasten the birth. Lewis decided to try it. He mixed two rings of a rattlesnake's tail with a little water and gave it to Sacagawea. Within 10 minutes, her baby was born. Lewis wasn't sure if it was the Indian remedy that had done the trick, but he was glad to see the healthy baby boy. Jean Baptiste Charbonneau was the baby's lengthy given name, but the boy was soon nicknamed "Pomp" and became a great favorite among the men of the Corps.

In time the days became longer. The icy river broke with loud cracks and creaks. Everyone's thoughts turned to the year ahead. Lewis finished his reports for Jefferson and packed crates full of marvels to send to the president. The men felled trees and hollowed them out with their axes to make six dugout canoes. Others put finishing touches on the repairs to the keelboat. They packed gear and dried buffalo meat. The men sang as they worked, happy to feel the sun and the spring wind. "All the party in high spirits," wrote Clark. They worked hard all day and danced and talked late into the night.

The Indians worked along the rising riverbanks, for the cold rushing waters carried trees useful for building lodges and buffalo that had been drowned in the strong currents. They jumped from one small chunk of ice to another to reach the buffalo, a very great risk in the cold spring currents. They set fires on both sides of the river to burn off the dry grasses and encourage new green shoots for their horses and the buffalo herds.

Another spring tradition among the Mandan was to visit their Medicine Stone, a large stone several days' journey from their villages. A ceremony was held at the stone, then the visitors slept nearby for the night. In the morning, they returned to the stone to read white marks that had appeared on it during the night. These marks told them of events to come in the year ahead, such as whether they would go to war or have peace.

April 7, 1805
The expedition leaves Fort Mandan and part of the expedition returns to St. Louis

The keelboat was packed and made ready for Corporal Warfington and the boatmen to travel back to St. Louis. It was full of marvelous surprises for President Jefferson. There were dried flowers, plants, and roots, all carefully labeled and described by Lewis. Boxes were packed with skeletons and fossils, animal skins and horns, insects, and mineral samples (including a pint of muddy Missouri River water!). Seeds from the Indians' corn, bean, and tobacco crops would be of great interest to the gardening president. So would the bows and arrows, painted buffalo robes, and deer-

Gifts from the Great West

President Jefferson created an "Indian Hall" in his home, Monticello, where he proudly displayed the antlers and Indian artifacts he received from the expedition. He sent the minerals and dozens of plant specimens to the American Philosophical Society. He kept some of the cuttings and seeds from the collection, and the next year he grew Arikara corn and beans in his garden. One of the magpies and the prairie dog made their new home at the American Philosophical Society and were visited by crowds of curious people.

skin dresses. Five live magpies and a sharp-tailed grouse were sent back east on the keelboat, along with the little prairie dog that the men had worked so hard to catch. Clark sent a map, the document he'd worked on all winter, showing the amazing new world they had entered. Lewis and Clark sent detailed reports of the Indians they had met and the "Most Remarkable Places" they had explored.

Warfington and his crew turned the keelboat downriver. The Corps of Discovery climbed into the six new dugouts and its two pirogues. They pointed the boats to the west. The Corps now included some new members, including the young woman, Sacagawea, and her baby, Pomp, wrapped up snugly and carried on his mother's back in a cradleboard. They waved goodbye to their Indian hosts and paddled upstream.

The expedition had traveled as far up the Missouri River as any bold fur trader had ever ventured. Beyond this point was unmapped territory. Lewis wrote in his journal before he went to sleep that night: "We were now about to penetrate a country at least two thousand miles in width, on which the foot of civilized man had never trodden. . . . I could but esteem this moment of my departure as among the most happy of my life."

Mother and child

5

Beautifull in the Extreme

April 1805
Farewell, Fort Mandan

The explorers were happy to be on the river again after the long winter at Fort Mandan. All were "in excellent health and spirits," Lewis noted. "Not a whisper or murmur of discontent to be heard among them, but all act in unison and with the most perfect harmony." Sacagawea was returning to her homeland with hopes for a happy reunion with her people. She had been taken from her family when the Hidatsa had raided her village years before. She had never dreamed she'd be returning on a voyage such as this one. Lewis's dog, Seaman, was glad to be out again. He walked along the shore with Lewis, sniffing the fresh smells of spring.

New grass covered the prairie. Thousands of geese stopped to feed on the tender shoots. Clark found a hare cloaked half in his coat of winter white and half in summer gray. Lewis noted the croaking choruses of frogs.

With the spring weather came strong winds. Windblown sand was in everyone's hair, eyes, and food. Their small boats tossed in the river's high waves. On some days they made no progress at all against the heavy winds. On those days they gave up and made camp. When the wind was with them, they raised sails to hurry the boats along.

On most days, paddling and pulling from dawn to dark, the expedition advanced 15 or 20 miles. At night the men slept under the stars after a hearty meal provided by the hunters. The captains shared a tipi with York, Charbonneau, Sacagawea, and Pomp.

They saw many buffalo that had drowned in the high waters of the river. Lewis inspected enormous tracks near them. They were the tracks of the "white bear." The Indians had told them about these animals. Lewis was anxious to meet one of the giant bears, in spite of the Indians' stories of their strength and ferocity. When the Indians prepared to hunt this animal, they painted themselves as if going on the warpath against a respected enemy.

Bald eagles flew overhead in large numbers. Lewis noted swans and owls. One day Clark saw a

Junction of the Yellowstone and Missouri Rivers

bird with a six-inch curved beak that whistled its name at him—"curlew, curlew." White whooping cranes, their black-tipped wings spreading seven feet across, flew overhead with long, slow beats.

The Corps saw beaver dens everywhere, and at night, when the camp became quiet, they heard the beavers' tails slapping the water. One night Lewis wrote about a buffalo calf that was afraid of Seaman and attached itself to Lewis, following close to his heels all day. When Lewis climbed above the river's high bluffs, he looked over green rolling hills and saw immense herds of buffalo, elk, deer, and antelope. Though game was plentiful and sometimes quite tame, the men only killed as much as they needed for food.

April 26, 1805
The Corps reaches the junction of the Yellowstone and Missouri Rivers

After several weeks of travel, the explorers knew from the Indians' descriptions that they would be coming to a fork in the river. One morning Lewis decided to walk ahead of the boats to search for it. He brought Seaman (who'd been out all night on an escapade but was always ready for a hike) and four of the men. In a short time they found the fork where two great rivers came together—the Missouri and the Yellowstone.

The view from a hill showed the wide valleys the two rivers had created, the lines of trees along their banks, and an abundance of grazing animals. Lewis and his men camped that night next to a new

river, the Yellowstone. In the morning Lewis sent Private Joseph Field to explore this river as far as he could walk in one day. He set the other men to work while he took measurements of latitude and longitude and collected plants. Captain Clark and the boats came up later, and everyone was happy to have reached the landmark. Field returned to report on his findings, which included a sighting of strange, big-horned animals. The Corps celebrated with a big meal and a drink for all. The sounds of fiddle music and song filled the night.

The Corps continued its journey up the Missouri River. A few days past the fork they encountered the "white bears" they'd heard so much about. That morning as they walked onshore, Lewis and one of the privates suddenly came face-to-face with two bears. They quickly raised their guns and fired. One of the bears escaped. The other, though badly wounded, chased after Lewis. Somehow Lewis was able to reload his gun and fire again. Lewis described the animal in detail in his journal. The bear's thick fur was brown. The Indians called it a white bear because its brown fur was tipped with white on the ends, giving it a "grizzled" (grayish) appearance. Lewis had killed a grizzly bear, an animal previously unknown to science. He described its long claws and teeth and marveled at the strength it had shown.

In the same journal entry he described other animals they'd seen that day, so many they could hardly look in any direction without seeing a deer, elk, or buffalo. Captain Clark had seen several big-horned animals. The creatures, bighorn sheep, ran nimbly along the sides of the steep cliffs that now lined the riverbanks. They would see more of these shy and agile animals as the days passed. The regal

Standing five feet tall, the magnificent whooping crane is North America's tallest bird. It is almost entirely white, with long black legs, black tips on its wings, and a red patch of skin on its head. Hunting and loss of habitat have greatly affected the whooping crane population, and at one time there were only 21 whooping cranes left in the wild.

In the spring, adult whoopers travel far to northern wetlands to lay their eggs in large nests. The mother and father take turns feeding their single baby, which is covered with brown feathers. The newborn crane grows rapidly, and in just over two months is ready to fly 2,400 miles to its winter home on the Gulf of Mexico. The whooping crane is named for its trumpeting whoop, which can be heard from two miles mile away, and is best known for its elaborate mating dance. The males and females, which mate for life, dance together, jumping up and down with wings outstretched, bowing their heads on their long necks.

Shall We Dance?

The Whooping Crane Waltz

In an effort to encourage the endangered whooping cranes to breed, one scientist learned to perform the whooping crane mating dance with the birds. Try the whooping crane waltz.

Materials

➡ *A partner*

Pretend to be a pair of whooping cranes facing each other across a field. One of you starts the dance by bowing your head and flapping your wings. Then leap high into the air and throw your head back so you're looking straight up to the sky. Your partner runs toward you with wings flapping and head bobbing. Jump up and down in unison, throwing your heads back to the sky. Back off from each other and bow again. Stretch your wings out and jump up and down some more. End the dance with an elegant bow!

The Sharp-Tailed Shake

During the springtime the plains were a lively place. Sharp-tailed grouse gathered at their dancing grounds (called "leks") in the dark right before dawn. Here they executed their magnificent courting displays, proud dances the males performed to win a bride. Some Indian societies dance like the grouse—you can too! Get ready for the sharp-tailed shake.

Materials

➡ *Chalk*
➡ *A partner*
➡ *Dance rattles (see Chapter 3 for instructions on making your own)*

Draw a circle on a patch of dirt or on the sidewalk with some chalk. One dancer runs into the circle and is joined by the other dancer. Lift your arms up, lower your head, and stoop over with your behind jutting out. Shuffle your feet back and forth and make a cooing sound while shaking your dance rattles. (The grouse makes a rattling noise by shaking its tail quills.) Approach each other, face-to-face, and slowly lower your heads more. Lower your bodies to the ground and end the dance spread out flat with your noses touching!

males looked down on the boats, their huge horns curving around their heads. It was marvelous to see them, some as large as 300 pounds, leaping along cliffs where no other creatures could find a foothold. Farther upstream, they saw so many porcupines that they named a river for them. It's a good thing Seaman didn't try to catch one of these creatures, for the porcupine is protected with 30,000 quills! When attacked, it tucks its head under its forepaws, raises its quills, and turns its tail on the attacker. The quills in the tail come out easily, so Seaman would have ended up with a nose full of long quills.

The beauty of the country was overwhelming. Lewis described it as "beautifull in the extreme." They began to see more trees along the banks of the river, which meandered from one high bluff to another. Every day brought a new adventure. Two of the hunters saw a mountain lion devouring a deer. One day Clark found a den of baby wolves. He and Drouillard also met a giant grizzly bear. They killed the animal, but not without danger and difficulty. It roared terribly when they wounded it and swam halfway across the river. This bear weighed nearly 600 pounds and measured eight and a half feet tall.

The next day when a grizzly swam across the river right in front of their boats, they let it go. "The curiosity of our party is pretty well satisfied with respect to this animal," Lewis said. They now understood the Indians' respect for the "white bear." They met several more over the next weeks. One bear ran after two hunters. When they jumped off a 20-foot bluff into the river, the bear jumped right in after them and almost caught one of the men before it was shot by another hunter on shore.

One day the captains walked together along the shore, making an exception to their policy that one of them should always be with the boats. They came to regret it. Charbonneau was steering one of the pirogues, and a strong gust of wind nearly turned the boat over. The captains were horrified. The pirogue contained their priceless journals and medicines and supplies that they couldn't live without. Several people in the boat could not swim, including little Pomp. Lewis nearly tore his coat off and jumped into the icy, wild waters. Realizing he could never reach the boat in time, he and Clark shot their guns to get the attention of those on board and shouted instructions to them.

Charbonneau was in a state of panic, crying out and waving his hands in the air. One of the men on board, Pierre Cruzatte, threatened to shoot him if he didn't pay attention to the rudder and right the boat. The sound of the captains' shots brought Charbonneau to his senses and he turned back to his job. Cruzatte and two others grabbed kettles and bailed the water out of the pirogue as quickly as they could. Everyone was shouting. It was a desperate moment. In the middle of it all, Sacagawea stayed calm. Though the boat had filled to its rim with water and nearly capsized, the young mother had the presence of mind to reach into the water and retrieve precious medicines and papers that were floating away.

Clark was fond of Sacagawea, whom he called Janey. After this incident Lewis wrote of her courage and steadiness. They were less impressed with Charbonneau! Sacagawea had proved to be a fortunate addition to the Corps. Her knowledge of wild plants was also helpful. She gathered prairie turnips, wild licorice, and berries to add to the meat

Big Bears

Clark guessed that the grizzly bear he shot weighed 500 pounds. Lewis thought it was 600. That seems huge, but at least one grizzly has weighed in at 1,500 pounds. Grizzlies stand 7 to 10 feet tall on their hind legs and four feet at the shoulder when on all fours. Amazingly, when they are born, grizzlies are tiny, blind cubs weighing only a half pound. They do not leave the den for months, then they follow their mother over the next two years to learn how to fish and hunt for berries. They eat all summer and fall then find a cave or hollow log to den up in for the winter. Grizzlies are big, but they are fast, too. They can run up to 40 miles an hour.

the hunters brought in for dinner. The captains named a river after their Shoshone friend.

Clark escaped another near disaster when he was almost bitten by a rattlesnake as he walked along the shore. That night there was a terrific storm. The man on guard woke the captains when he saw that the tree next to their tipi was leaning dangerously in the wind. The captains, York, Char-

Hunting the grizzly bear

bonneau, and Sacagawea quickly broke down the tipi and moved it. Minutes later the tree crashed down on the place where the tipi had been. "We should have been crushed to atoms," Lewis said.

One day Seaman swam out in the river to fetch a beaver that had been shot by a hunter. The beaver was still alive and bit Seaman on the leg. As Lewis bandaged up the terrible wound, he wondered if his dog would survive, but within weeks Seaman was well enough to save the explorers' lives. One night as they slept, a buffalo, confused in the darkness, crashed through camp. It came within inches of crushing several of the men. They were saved just in time by Seaman, who rushed at the buffalo, barked wildly, and chased it away.

As the explorers traveled on, the hills on either side of the river grew higher. The wind still blew hard and the men frequently had to resort to towing the boats. "Their labor is incredibly painful and great," wrote Lewis, "yet those faithful fellows bear it without a murmur." Their elkskin ropes broke, the stones in the river's bottom cut their feet, and the icy currents chilled them. The air was still cold, too, and though it was spring the ground was frosty when they woke up in the mornings. But the air was clean and fresh, and the land unfolding before them was a scene of wonder.

One afternoon, Lewis climbed a hill and gazed off toward the horizon. He could see distant mountains ahead, their snow-covered peaks shining in the late-day sun. He was thrilled at the sight. Moments later, as he thought of the difficulties this "snowey barrier" could cause his men, he became troubled. But he wrote in his journal, "As I have always held it a crime to anticipate evils I will believe it a good comfortable road untill I am compelled to believe differently."

Lewis was looking ahead, but at least for a moment, Clark was looking back. When they reached a clear and beautiful stream flowing into the Missouri, Clark thought it a lovely sight. "Judith's River" he called the stream, for Julia (Judy) Hancock, a young Virginian woman who had captured his heart.

On the same day, they found the remains of a recent Indian encampment. Sacagawea looked at a moccasin left behind at the site and shook her head—it was not left by her Shoshone people. A little farther on they came to the base of a tall cliff and found the bones of many dead buffalo. It was the site of a "pishkun," or buffalo jump. Indians sometimes hunted buffalo by herding them off cliffs. A young man disguised as a buffalo would stand between the herd and a cliff. Other hunters surrounded the herd then ran toward it. The disguised hunter ran ahead of the buffalo toward the cliff and at the last minute jumped onto a safe projection or hid in a crevice he'd selected beforehand. The animals would blindly follow and fall to their deaths. It was a very dangerous trick, and only the fastest hunters were chosen for the hunt. The captains named a stream near this place Slaughter Creek.

The country the Corps traveled through was a land of "visionary inchantment." The river cut its way through hills of white sandstone. The bright rock of the hills had been carved by water and wind into strange, towering shapes that reminded the men of columns and elaborate buildings. Bighorn sheep looked down on them, and swallows flew overhead from their nests in the cliffs.

June 2, 1805
The Corps reaches the junction of the Missouri and Maria's Rivers

One day the explorers were surprised to find themselves at the junction of two great rivers. The captains had misunderstood the distances described by the Hidatsa chiefs. They thought they had already passed a river the Hidatsa called "The River Which Scolds All Others" and now did not know that one of these was the "scolding" river. They were confused and didn't know which way to go. Which river was the Missouri?

The captains faced a big decision and couldn't afford to make a mistake. If they chose the wrong river, they might not discover their mistake for some time. They could lose valuable weeks and months. A wrong turn could mean losing the whole season, could require a forced winter camp, and could perhaps even end their expedition! They camped at the fork and set out to discover which river was the Missouri.

The explorers looked carefully at each of the rivers. The south branch was wider, faster, and more shallow. Its waters were clear and it had a rocky bottom. The north branch had a muddy bottom. It ran deep, and its waters were brown like those of the Missouri River, on which they'd traveled for so long. All of the privates were positive that the north branch was the Missouri, but the captains disagreed. They should be close to the source of the Missouri River by now, they thought. That source should be in the mountains ahead, which meant the river should be running clearer and faster, like the south branch. Because the north branch was muddy, the captains thought its source must be far away and that it was muddy because of all of the soil it had collected while running over miles of open plain. However, the captains agreed it was best to investigate. Clark would explore the south branch while Lewis explored the north.

Captain Clark's explorations took him 40 miles upstream. This river was running so swiftly that even the buffalo he saw couldn't cross it. He and his men camped, killed three grizzly bears that

Driving buffalo off a cliff

A Buffalo Mask

Make this buffalo mask to wear or hang from a wall.

Materials

- *Several pieces of heavy 9-by-12-inch construction paper*
- *Pencil*
- *Scissors*
- *Ruler*
- *Glue*
- *Tape*
- *Stapler*
- *½-inch wide elastic, 12 inches long*

1. On a sheet of construction paper that will be the buffalo's face, draw two large eyes, then cut them out.
2. From another sheet, cut out a nose that is 2½ inches wide at the top and 1½ inches wide at the bottom and has 3½-inch long sides. Fold a ½-inch margin along each

Nose

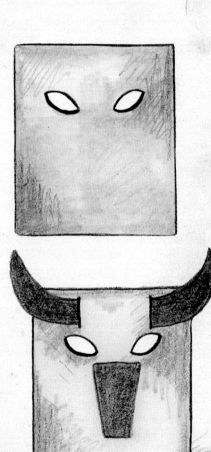

side, then bend them back. Apply glue to the ½-inch margins and affix the nose to the mask.

3. Cut out two curved horns approximately 5 inches long. Carefully cut two vertical slits in the mask above the outside edge of the eyes. Insert the horns into these slots, then tape them down on the back.

4. For the beard, cut out a 3-by-3½-inch rectangle. Cut the rectangle into very thin strips, leaving a ¼-inch margin at one long end (see drawing). Apply glue to one side of the ¼-inch margin and affix the beard to the buffalo's chin.

5. For hair, cut out a 4½-by 3-inch rectangle. Cut this rectangle into very thin strips, leaving a ¼-inch margin at one end. Apply glue to one side of the ¼-inch margin and affix the hair to the buffalo's forehead.

6. Cut the mask along each side at an angle, so that it is widest at the base of the eyes and narrowest at the chin (see drawing).

7. Staple the elastic to the mask on each side at about eye level. Now your mask is ready to wear.

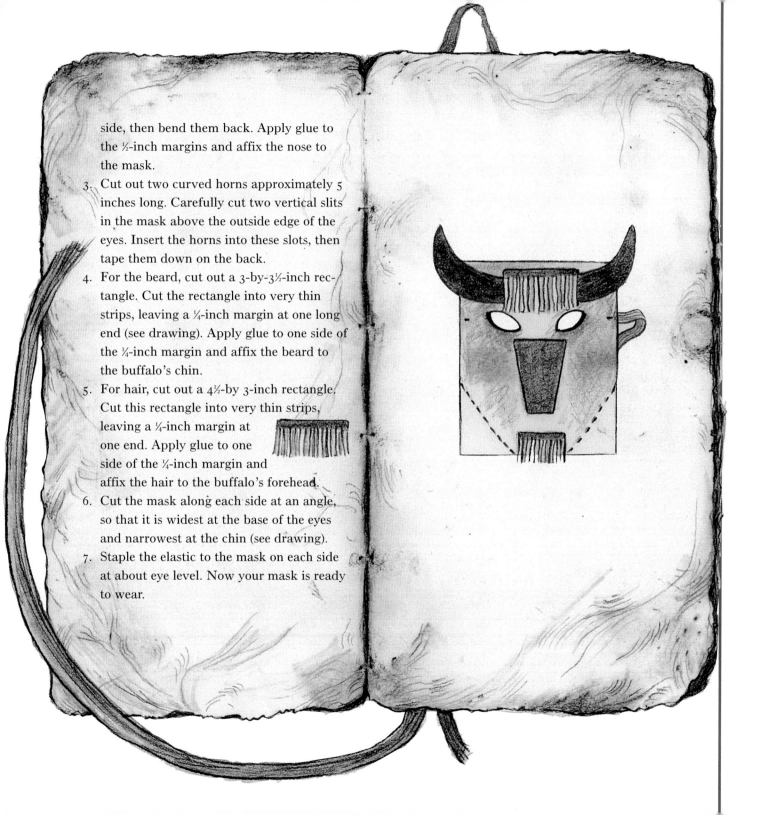

Great Falls of the Missouri

broke in on their campsite, and returned three days later to wait for Lewis's report.

Lewis was gone five days. He traveled 60 miles up the river before he came to the conclusion that its direction was taking him too far to the north. He and his men turned around. Lewis and Private Richard Windsor made their way back on the side of a cliff, picking their way carefully along a narrow ledge. Lewis slipped and nearly fell down the face of the 90-foot cliff. Quick use of his espontoon saved him. As he was catching his breath, he heard his companion calling out for help. Windsor had slipped and fallen, too! His right arm and leg were hanging off the cliff and he was barely holding onto the ledge with his left hand and foot. He was terrified. Lewis was frightened, too, and unable to reach Windsor. He managed to tell him very calmly that he was in no danger. All he would have to do, Lewis instructed, was take his knife out of its holder with his right hand and dig a hole in the face of the cliff for his foot. Windsor did as the captain suggested and soon was able to make the foothold and push himself back onto the ledge.

When the captains reunited, they agreed that the south branch was the real Missouri River. Lewis named the north branch for a beloved cousin. Even though the river was muddy and his cousin was "lovely and fair," Lewis said it was a noble river and he named it "Maria's River." The captains discussed their decision to follow the south branch with the Corps. All of the men still believed the north branch was the Missouri, but every one of them cheerfully agreed to follow the leaders. Because their men were so convinced that the north branch was the Missouri River, Lewis and Clark decided that a small party should walk ahead. The Hidatsa had told them that they would come upon a great waterfall along the Missouri River. Once they found the falls, they could be certain they'd made the right choice. Lewis would hike ahead; Clark would follow with the party in the boats.

They decided to "cache" (store in a hidden spot) some of the things they wouldn't need right away so that when they came to the falls, they wouldn't have to carry so much overland. They could pick everything up again on their return trip. The men dug a deep hole and lined the bottom with dry sticks. They filled it with specimens they had collected, clothes, and extra ammunition, and covered it all with an animal skin, then with dirt and leaves. They hid one of the pirogues on an island.

Lewis packed a few things and chose four men to accompany him. He wasn't feeling well as they set off on their hike. They hunted along the way and hung the meat up in trees for Clark to pick up as he brought the boats upriver. Lewis couldn't eat. He grew feverish and was in great pain. Remembering his mother's teachings, he had his men gather chokecherry twigs. He boiled them up and drank the bitter tea, and the next day, he was well enough to hike 27 miles.

June 13, 1805
Lewis and his companions discover the Great Falls of the Missouri River

As he hiked ahead of his men, Lewis heard a roaring sound. His heart leaped. Could it be the waterfall? He saw spray in the air "like a column of smoke" and hurried his steps. Soon he came upon the source of the roar. Of all the wonderful things Lewis had seen, this waterfall was "the grandest sight," he said, that "I ever beheld." The wide river plunged over an 80-foot cliff, crashing on the rocks below and sending jets of foam straight up in the air. The water billowed and swirled and surged. A beautiful rainbow arced through the mist and spray.

The next morning, Lewis sent Private Joseph Field back to find Clark and tell him the good news—they'd chosen the right river! In the meantime, Lewis walked ahead to see how far they would have to "portage" (transport their canoes overland). After a few miles he was surprised to come upon another waterfall. Hearing a roaring sound ahead, he pushed on farther and found another. A few miles distant there was yet another. Soon he found a fifth. He spent some time wondering which was the most beautiful and concluded that while one was "pleasingly beautifull, the other was sublimely grand." At the base of the last waterfall, on an island in the middle of the river, an eagle had built its nest. The Hidatsa had said to look for this nest in the middle of the stream. Lewis knew he was in the right place.

On his return to camp, Lewis hunted a buffalo for that night's dinner. He shot his gun, and before he had a chance to reload, he was attacked by a grizzly bear! The bear charged him at full speed, its mouth open. Lewis ran; the bear ran faster. Lewis jumped into the river and the bear plunged in after him. Lewis realized his only chance was to attack. Waist deep in water, he lunged at the bear with his espontoon, and the grizzly, taken by surprise at this turn of events, wheeled around and withdrew.

It was late and Lewis was exhausted, but his day wasn't over yet. Lewis headed back to join his men and encountered a mountain lion, crouched and ready to spring on him. He shot and missed, but he finally drove the cat away. No sooner did he get past this danger than three bull buffalo ran at him at full speed. "All the beasts of the neighbourhood had made a league to distroy me," he wrote. He was very relieved to get back to camp safely. The next morning his adventures still weren't over—he woke to find a large rattlesnake only a few feet from his head!

Clark and the rest of the party worked to get the boats up the swift river. Clark was glad to see Private Field, both because of Field's good news about the falls and because Clark was anxious to reach Lewis's camp. Sacagawea was sick, and all of Clark's efforts to help her had come to nothing. He had bled her (a common medical practice of the day), making a cut on her arm and letting the blood flow. Sacagawea was getting worse every day, and Clark worried that she might die.

She refused to take any more medicine, and Charbonneau, anxious for his wife, wanted to return to the Hidatsa.

By the time Lewis saw her, Sacagawea was extremely ill. She was feverish and in pain, and her arms and fingers twitched. He worried for the young woman, for her infant Pomp, and for the fate of the party without her. He treated her with bark tea and made her drink water from a sulfur spring.

Under his care, and to everyone's great relief, Sacagawea quickly got better.

While Lewis tended Sacagawea, Clark surveyed the land ahead to find the best route for their portage. They would have to carry all their goods and the boats overland for 18 miles to reach a place where the river was smooth again and the banks low. The captains decided to make another cache and leave the second pirogue hidden. The men cut down a cottonwood tree to make wagons and wheels. They loaded their dugout canoes and their supplies onto the wagons and started the portage.

The explorers made four trips in 11 days. It took all of their strength to pull the wagons across the broken land. The ground was covered with prickly pears, which pierced their moccasins and their feet. The men bent low to the ground, grasping stones and plants to pull themselves forward. At each halt they collapsed, exhausted. On some days it was terrifically hot. On other days there were violent storms. One day hail the size of their fists beat down on their unprotected heads and shoulders. Clark, Charbonneau, Sacagawea, and Pomp took cover under a rock shelf in a dry ravine. Rain fell in torrents, and soon the ravine filled with a raging flood. Clark pushed Sacagawea up over a ledge while the water rose around his waist.

The explorers made a camp at the end of the portage and named it White Bear Islands for the large number of grizzlies that lived there. Buffalo also gathered there in huge herds. (Clark counted 10,000!) Here they celebrated another Fourth of July. They divided the last rations of whiskey and danced to Cruzatte's fiddle. Though exhausted by their long days, they found it hard to sleep at night. The buffalo bulls roared, and grizzly bears prowled the camp. Seaman barked and growled all night in his efforts to drive the animals away.

While some of the men finished carrying the goods overland, others began preparing elk and buffalo skins to cover the special iron-frame boat they had brought all the way from the east. This boat, when finished, would take the place of the two pirogues they had cached. They covered the frame with the skins and sewed them together. When they launched the boat, it "lay like a perfect cork on the water," but in a short time it began to leak. It was a terrible disappointment. Ahead were the snow-covered mountains they would have to cross before winter. Time was running short.

Rather than go back for the two pirogues, the men cut down two giant cottonwood trees, hollowed them out, and made large dugout canoes.

Make Your Own Moccasins

On prickly pear country, a pair of moccasins only lasted two days. The men of the Corps made moccasins by the dozens!

Materials

Moccasins

- → Scissors
- → Brown paper bag
- → Pencil
- → Ruler
- → 1 yard of felt
- → Pins
- → Needle
- → Thread
- → Beads, store-bought or homemade

Homemade "Beads"

- → Water
- → Cups
- → Food coloring
- → Salad macaroni
- → Spoon
- → Newspaper

1. Cut the brown paper bag and spread it out flat. Step on it. Measure four inches out from your foot in every direction and draw an outline of this big foot. Repeat with your other foot. These will be the patterns for your moccasins.

Brown paper bag

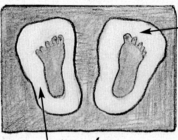

4 inches

4 inches

2. Pin the patterns to the felt and cut the felt in the shape of the big foot.

Cut off felt

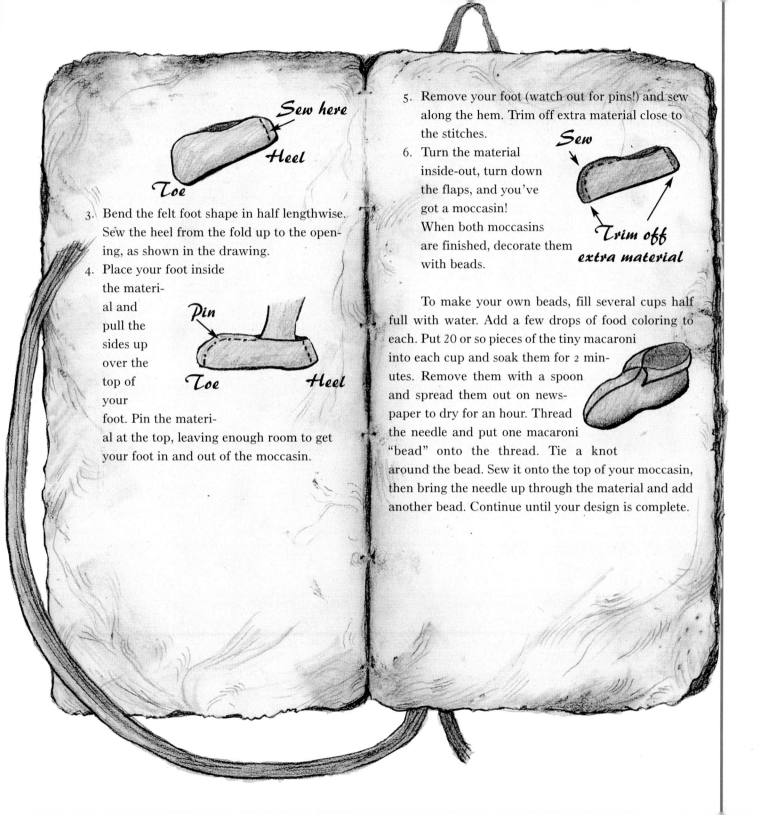

Sew here

Heel

Toe

3. Bend the felt foot shape in half lengthwise. Sew the heel from the fold up to the opening, as shown in the drawing.

4. Place your foot inside the material and pull the sides up over the top of your foot. Pin the material at the top, leaving enough room to get your foot in and out of the moccasin.

Pin

Toe   **Heel**

5. Remove your foot (watch out for pins!) and sew along the hem. Trim off extra material close to the stitches.

6. Turn the material inside-out, turn down the flaps, and you've got a moccasin! When both moccasins are finished, decorate them with beads.

Sew

Trim off extra material

To make your own beads, fill several cups half full with water. Add a few drops of food coloring to each. Put 20 or so pieces of the tiny macaroni into each cup and soak them for 2 minutes. Remove them with a spoon and spread them out on newspaper to dry for an hour. Thread the needle and put one macaroni "bead" onto the thread. Tie a knot around the bead. Sew it onto the top of your moccasin, then bring the needle up through the material and add another bead. Continue until your design is complete.

They dried buffalo meat for the journey ahead, repaired their tattered clothes, and made new moccasins. They cached the iron frame, more of Lewis's plant specimens, and Clark's latest map.

After 10 days, the Corps was ready to move on. Though the snow-peaked mountains ahead looked forbidding, Lewis noted proudly that his men appeared to have "made up their minds to succeed in the expedition or perish in the attempt." They put their boats in the river and headed upstream. Lewis was happy to walk along the shore again. Though the prickly pear made for difficult hiking, it was beautiful in full bloom. Sunflowers too were "in blume and abundant."

6

Tab-ba-bone and So-So-Ne

July 18, 1805
The Corps of Discovery passes through the Gates of the Rocky Mountains

The river flowed past towering rocky cliffs that dwarfed the canoes. At every turn it looked as if huge boulders would tumble down on them. Lewis called the "dark and gloomy" river canyon they passed through "The Gates of the Rocky Mountains." It didn't seem possible that anything could live on the steep cliffs, but the explorers saw dozens of bighorn sheep jumping from rock to rock, with no concern for the sheer drops beneath them.

The river here was swift. For many days, the men pulled the boats with towlines. Seaman splashed along beside them, sometimes catching an unsuspecting goose. Past the towering cliffs they came into a beautiful valley ringed by ranges of high, snow-covered mountains. Sacagawea recognized this country. She had been here with her people, the Shoshone, she told Lewis, and soon they would come to a place where the river divided into three. Everyone was happy to hear this news, for it meant they were close to the Shoshone and perhaps would make it over the mountains before winter set in.

July 25, 1805
The Corps reaches the Three Forks of the Missouri River

The captains decided that a small party should walk ahead in search of the Indians. While Lewis and the rest of the party struggled with the boats, Clark and three men hiked ahead. They saw smoke in the distance and wondered if it was a signal. Perhaps it was about them! They hoped it was a Shoshone hunting party, but Clark and his men saw only old signs of the Indians—a trail, an abandoned village, and a wild horse.

One day they came to three forks in the river. Clark looked at each stream and decided to follow the fork to the right. It seemed to come most directly from the mountains to the west. He wrote a note for Lewis explaining his decision and stuck it on to a tree branch.

When Lewis arrived, he found the note and called to his men to make camp. They spent a couple of days at the three forks, and during this time Lewis named the rivers—the Madison (for the secretary of state), the Gallatin (for the secretary of the

treasury), and the Jefferson. Sacagawea knew this place. Here the Hidatsa war party had fallen upon her tribe and taken her prisoner. She had tried to escape by swimming across the river but had been captured midstream. She must have been having many thoughts now that she was back at this place, but she didn't show them to the men.

When Clark returned, he reported spotting a great number of beaver and otter, but he had seen no sign at all of Indians. The captains were growing anxious. Everything depended on the Shoshones. The expedition needed help, directions, and horses.

After a rest, the explorers proceeded up the fork named the Jefferson River. This time Lewis walked ahead. He came upon two more branches of the river and named one Wisdom and the other Philanthropy, two qualities he thought President Jefferson possessed. Lewis decided that the Jefferson was the right river to follow and left a note for Clark on a tree near this fork.

After investigating the country upriver, Lewis returned to meet the boats. When they didn't appear, he was worried, but soon he heard whoops and hollers coming from another direction. Clark and the Corps had gone up the wrong stream and had had one misadventure after another, with canoes overturning, one man nearly drowning, and supplies spilling into the water. Lewis wondered how Clark could have missed his note. Clark had seen nothing. The mystery was solved when the captains realized that one of the many beavers living on the stream had chopped down the tree that had held Lewis's message.

The Beaver

The beaver's appetite for trees is huge. One beaver family can cut down 200 aspen and cottonwood trees every year. They drag them to the water, where they float the logs to their homes. They bury the trees under stones on the river bottom, and, when they're hungry for a snack, dive down, retrieve some wood, and bring it home to eat.

Beavers also use trees to build dams and lodges. These structures are amazing feats of animal engineering. Branches, sticks, and mud are anchored across streams to build watertight dams, then the beavers build lodges in the quiet ponds that form behind the dams. The lodges can be very large (25 feet long and rising 8 feet above the water's surface). Deep inside, the beavers live on platforms built above the water level where they can stay dry and cozy. Like our homes, the lodges have different rooms for eating, sleeping, and storing food. Their entrances are below the water level, making it impossible for predators (such as bears and wolves) to enter. Lewis and Clark also saw beavers living in dens along the river's bank.

The beaver is the largest rodent in North America, weighing up to

August 8, 1805
Sacagawea recognizes Beaver's Head Rock, a sign that the Corps is near the home of the Shoshone

Once they were back on the right river, the explorers' passage upstream grew more difficult with every mile. The river twisted and became so shallow that the boats scraped on the rocky bottom. Several of the men, including Clark, were sick. Shannon had gone out on a hunt and was once again missing. The Shoshone tribe seemed a distant dream. Sacagawea brightened everyone's spirits when she pointed to a hill she called the Beaver's Head and informed them that her people stayed near this place.

With this news, the captains decided that Lewis should walk ahead and find Sacagawea's people. He intended to follow the stream to its source in the mountains, cross the mountains, and find the Columbia River—and the Shoshone. He hoped to find an easy portage route, perhaps a day's journey over the mountains' and then a new river, the Columbia, to take them to the ocean.

Beaver lodge

August 13, 1805
Lewis meets the Shoshone

Lewis packed his things and set out with three companions, just as, to everyone's relief, Shannon returned to the company. Lewis and the men hiked in the direction of the Beaver's Head and within a few days came upon a trail. It wound over the shoulders of the mountains and down into narrow valleys. Shortly after, they saw an Indian in the distance, mounted on a horse and looking their way. Lewis was thrilled and quickened his pace; the Indian urged his horse toward them. As they grew closer, Lewis took out a robe, unfurled it, and laid it on the ground, a sign of friendship he'd learned from Sacagawea. He set down his gun and walked forward, crying out a word he'd also learned from the Shoshone woman, "Tab-ba-bone!" But it was the wrong word. Lewis thought he was saying the Shoshone word for white man but he was actually saying the word for stranger. This did nothing to reassure the lone Indian, who turned his horse and galloped away.

Lewis and his companions tried to follow the young man but failed. A rainstorm came on that quickly erased his horse's tracks. The explorers camped for the night. The next day they saw more signs of Indians—old twig-and-brush lodges, the tracks of horses, and holes dug by root gatherers. The trail took them into the mountains, where the explorers found a spring, (water that comes from beneath the ground). Lewis wrote that they had arrived at "the most distant fountain of the waters of the Mighty Missouri." The expedition had made a long and difficult journey to reach this place. "Judge then of the pleasure I felt in allaying my thirst with this pure and ice-cold water," Lewis said. Private McNeal stood with one foot on each side of the little stream and said he was delighted to be able to straddle the river they had struggled up for so long.

A few miles beyond the spring they came to a mountain pass. Here Lewis crossed the Continental Divide, the great ridge that divides the continent. Beyond this ridge, all rivers run to the west instead of the east. Standing on the ridge, Lewis lifted his eyes and saw "immence ranges of high mountains still to the West of us with their tops partially covered with snow." It wasn't going to be an easy crossing to the Columbia River after all. Range after range of high mountains were in their path. Lewis didn't let the sight dash his hopes.

There was much to think about, but for now Lewis had to find the Shoshone. The next day, to Lewis's joy, they met three Shoshone women who were out gathering food. One young woman ran away as the strangers approached. An old woman and the other young

Sacagawea

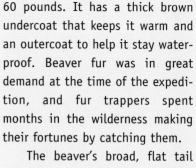

60 pounds. It has a thick brown undercoat that keeps it warm and an outercoat to help it stay waterproof. Beaver fur was in great demand at the time of the expedition, and fur trappers spent months in the wilderness making their fortunes by catching them.

The beaver's broad, flat tail serves many purposes. It acts as a rudder and an oar in the water and steadies the animal when it stands upright on its hind legs. When danger approaches, the beaver slaps its tail on the top of the water as a warning. The sound can be heard a mile away. The other beavers duck underwater, where they can stay 20 minutes before coming up for air.

Beavers mate for life and have two to four babies every spring. The babies, called "kits," can swim right away. They live with their family for two years before they go off to make their own dams and lodges elsewhere on the river.

83

woman froze in fear, lowering their heads as if they were ready to be taken prisoner. Lewis took one woman by the hand and lifted her to her feet. He gave both women small gifts of moccasins and mirrors to reassure them. He painted their cheeks with vermilion dye. One of Lewis's companions, Drouillard, spoke to them in Indian sign language. Just as he began to ask the women to take them to their village, a band of 60 Shoshone warriors appeared, riding their horses toward them at full speed!

The courageous Captain Lewis walked toward the warriors, and they slowed their horses. He approached the man in the lead. The old woman eagerly showed this man the presents Lewis had given to her. At this, the chief dismounted and embraced Lewis in friendship.

The chief, Cameahwait, welcomed Lewis and his men and brought them back to the Shoshone camp. They were treated with the greatest courtesy. They were seated on antelope skins inside a tipi while the women and children of the village clustered around, peeking inside. Cameahwait lit his pipe and pointed it in the four directions before presenting it to Lewis to smoke. The white men were given the only food the Indians had to eat—cakes of dried berries and a piece of salmon (a clue, Lewis thought, that the Pacific Ocean was close by). As well as he could in sign language, Drouillard explained their mission to the Shoshone chief, who must have been amazed at their story. It was the first time the Shoshone had ever seen white men.

Lewis and his men camped with the Shoshone that night. As the sun set, Lewis walked to the river with Cameahwait and Drouillard. The white men inquired, through signs, about the river—could they follow it to the great waters to the west?

Cameahwait's answer was discouraging. The river was too rapid and rocky as it passed through the high mountains, impossible to travel by boat or on foot along its banks. They would have to find another route over the mountains, then take to the waters again when they reached the other side. Cameahwait couldn't tell them where to cross, but an old man in his band, Toby, had some knowledge of the route and of the Indian tribe on the other side. These people, the Nez Perce, crossed the mountains every year to hunt for buffalo on the plains. But, Cameahwait warned, the route was difficult and treacherous.

August 17, 1805
Clark's party joins Lewis
and the Shoshone; Sacagawea
is reunited with her brother

The warning didn't stop Lewis. He noticed the hundreds of horses the Shoshone kept and believed if he could trade for some of them, the Corps could travel over the mountains. He asked Cameahwait to come back with him down the trail to meet Clark and the rest of his party and help them carry their supplies to the Indian camp. Though many of the Shoshone people believed that the white men were laying a trap for them, Cameahwait quickly agreed to join Lewis. He brought many of his people to help.

They recrossed the mountain pass, walking the miles with no food. The Shoshone were suffering. In previous years they had been able to hunt for buffalo in the plains, but lately their enemies, the

Speaking in Sign

Lewis wrote that Drouillard "understood perfectly the language of signs, which seems to be universally understood by all nations we have yet seen." This sign language common to the Plains tribes goes back hundreds of years. You can learn some of the signs Drouillard used to speak to the Shoshone!

BUFFALO: Make fists with both hands, leaving the index fingers pointing out and slightly curved. Bring your hands to either side of your forehead and tip your curved fingers forward like the buffalo's horns.

BEAR: Place your hands near your ears, palms facing forward and curve your fingers down so they look like round ears.

TIPI: Hold your hands in front of your chest facing each other. Touch your fingertips together and hold your palms far apart, making an angle shaped like a tipi.

SUN: With your left hand, make a semicircle with your thumb and index finger. Move your left hand in a curve from east to west.

MOON: Make a semicircle with the thumb and index finger of your left hand. Then make the sign for night by holding both hands, open and palms down, about one foot apart in front of you with the right hand higher than the left. Then cross your wrists, right over left.

MOUNTAIN: Make your hands into fists and raise them above your head. Then bring them down, one to each side of your chest, and move them forward very slowly (to demonstrate the great effort needed to climb a mountain).

HORSE: Hold your left hand in front of your chest with the palm facing the chest and the fingers straight. Straddle it with the index and middle fingers of your right hand.

THANK YOU: Hold both of your hands in front of you with palms down, then lower them down toward the ground.

FRIEND: Hold your right hand, palm facing forward, next to your right shoulder, with the index finger and middle finger straight up and together, and the other fingers closed.

Lewis and Clark meeting Indians at Ross' Hole

Blackfoot, Hidatsa, and other tribes, had raided their camps, and kept them from the hunt. Cameahwait's people were hungry. When Drouillard killed a deer, it was a welcome meal for all.

As they approached the place where Lewis hoped to meet Clark, Cameahwait stopped him. The chief placed his shawl of otter fur around Lewis's neck. Lewis took the hint and put his three-cornered hat on Cameahwait's head. If this was a trap, Lewis now looked like an Indian and would be the one killed.

It was a long, tense day and night, for Clark was nowhere in sight. When the boats finally appeared, Lewis heaved a sigh of relief. Walking in

the lead of Clark's party was Sacagawea with her little son. As the men shouted greetings, Sacagawea began to dance. She showed signs of "extravagant joy" and sucked on her fingers (a sign that the people she saw ahead were her tribe). As she came closer, a young woman ran out of the crowd and embraced her. This girl, Jumping Fish, had been Sacagawea's childhood friend. Both had been taken prisoner by the Hidatsa, but Jumping Fish had escaped. She must have thought that she would never see Sacagawea again.

Clark was introduced to Cameahwait, who greeted Clark by placing six small shells in the captain's hair. Lewis had the men set up an awning for a council. The captains, Cameahwait, and his chiefs had a smoke, then were ready to talk.

Captain Lewis sent for Sacagawea to interpret. She sat down with the men and began to translate Lewis's words. Suddenly she stopped and stared at the Shoshone chief, then jumped up, speechless with joy. The chief of the Shoshone tribe was her brother! Sacagawea ran to Cameahwait's side, threw her blanket over him, and held him, weeping. It took some time before she could find words again, and the happy young woman burst into tears several times while translating at the council. They stayed at this happy meeting place for several days, and called it Camp Fortunate.

Though Cameahwait had warned them that the river to the west was impassable, the captains decided that Clark would take a party, under the direction of Toby, to investigate this route. Lewis would see to it that their belongings were moved over the pass to the Shoshone encampment where he would begin to trade for horses. Within a few days of difficult hiking, Clark found that Cameah-

The Horse

Though the ancestors of the horse lived in North America millions of years ago, they became extinct on this continent and the earliest Americans did not have horses. In the 1500s Spanish explorers brought the horse back to the Americas. Over time, horses once again spread over the land, becoming a central part of Native American life on the Great Plains.

Having horses changed everything. Without horses, hunting was done on foot and was much more difficult. Hunting techniques such as the pishkun (in which buffalo were herded over a cliff) were used; nets and traps caught smaller game. People traveled on foot with dogs pulling the travois.

wait was right. The river was narrow, all rapids and falls, and bordered by steep mountains. Game was very scarce. Clark turned back to the Shoshone village. Toby offered to lead them across the mountains on a route to the north.

While waiting for Clark's return, Lewis had his men make willow nets, which they used to catch trout in the mountain stream. They cached some supplies and sunk their boats underwater, weighting them with stones to the river bottom, where they would be safe from fire. They made saddles out of boards and oars.

August 18, 1805
Happy Birthday, Lewis!

While making arrangements, Lewis noted that it was his 31st birthday. He wrote a birthday resolution in his journal, promising that he would use the talents that "nature and fortune had bestoed on me" to live for mankind and "advance the information of the succeeding generation."

The Corps stayed with the Shoshone for two weeks. The explorers traded coats, knives, and axes for horses and finished their preparations for the difficult mountain crossing. Of Sacagawea's family, only Cameahwait and a young nephew remained. The tribe had been devastated by raids. Many of the people had cut their hair short in mourning.

When times were better, the Shoshone people had caught fish in the spring and summer with spears and traps made of willow. They had

made bread of sunflower seeds and had eaten roots gathered by the women of the tribe. In the fall, they made long journeys to the east to hunt for buffalo, which provided meat for the winter and material for robes, moccasins, tools, weapons, and even halters for their horses. Their fringed shirts and dresses made of buffalo skin were decorated with dyed quills and precious seashells obtained in trade with tribes to the west.

The Shoshone had also made traps for smaller game and had made cloaks of otter and weasel fur. Cameahwait gave one of these cloaks to Lewis, and it became one of his proudest possessions. Some of the men wore otter skin bands around their heads, and had skunk tails trailing from their moccasins. They ornamented their hair and their horses' manes with eagle feathers. The most respected warriors wore bear-claw collars.

The raids had deprived the Shoshone of their lodges, and they were living in temporary shelters of willow and brush. In spite of their hardships, they were cheerful people, playful, open, and generous. Like the women of the Plains tribes, the Shoshone women were in charge of gathering fruits and roots, dressing buffalo skins and making clothes, and collecting wood and water. They made beautiful willow baskets with a weave so tight that the baskets held water.

The Shoshone men were responsible for hunting and for protecting their families. They brought home fish and game. Every man kept one horse near his lodge at all times and

Family in front of grass shelter

his weapons close by, ready to defend his people against attack. Though the Shoshone had suffered many raids, they still had hundreds of horses. One day Lewis watched as several men pursued an antelope herd. They posted their horses several miles apart, then one man set out on his horse, chasing the swift animals at full speed. When he reached the next hunter, that man gave chase to the herd on his fresh horse. In this way, they could wear the antelope down.

Lewis wrote detailed notes about Shoshone ways. He spelled their name as "So-So-Ne." Lewis and Clark also called them the Snake Indians, a name given to them by their Lakota enemies. Lewis described their bows made of the horns of elk and bighorn sheep. He wrote about a special ceremony to prepare a warrior's shield. He noted that the Shonshone seldom reprimanded their children. They considered bravery the most important quality and felt that punishment would break a youngster's spirit. Lewis and Clark thought highly of these people, who were "sincere in their friendship and kind with what they have to spare." Lewis shared some of the Corps's supplies with them, including corn, which the Shoshone had never tasted. He gave some dried squash from the Mandan villages to Cameahwait, who was delighted with this new treat. Sacagawea shared a taste of sugar with her brother, who declared it the best thing he'd ever tasted.

The Shoshone people, in turn, were very interested in the men of the Corps. Everything about them astonished the Indians, said Lewis, from the men and their weapons to the boats and the intelligence of Lewis's dog.

One day the Corps was ready to move on. The explorers had purchased 29 horses from the Shoshone and had packed them with their supplies. Toby and his son would serve as guides. Sacagawea lifted Pomp onto her shoulders as she told the Shoshone good-bye. The path ahead was through rough and wild, mountainous country. Cameahwait had warned them of its dangers and difficulties. But the captains were determined to reach their goal, and their men shared their resolve.

When the horse became part of their lives, hunting practices changed. Now hunters were able to kill buffalo with bows and arrows from horseback. They could get much more food for their families. Some settled agricultural tribes became nomadic hunting tribes. With horses pulling the travois, it was much easier to travel long distances.

The horse changed relations between tribes, the tribes that were rich in horses became the strongest. The Teton Sioux dominated the plains. Farther west, the Blackfoot had the most horses and were the most powerful. Wealth was based on possession of horses—the hand sign for "rich" is a combination of the signs for "much" and "horse." Taking horses from rival tribes was a bold and praiseworthy act.

Make a Basket

ative peoples made baskets of willow, cedar bark, beargrass, and pine needles. They used them for cooking, storage, and threshing. They used the same materials and techniques to weave fish traps, hats, mats, and cradles. Try your hand at basket-weaving.

Materials

- *2 six-yard lengths of twisted craft paper (available at craft and fabric stores)*
- *Scissors*

From one of the six-yard lengths of craft paper, cut three pieces, each 24 inches long. Use one piece to tie the other two together in the middle with a loose knot. Now cut a 12-inch piece of twisted paper and push it through the knot. Spread the pieces so they are all evenly spaced. These pieces will be the ribs of your basket.

Take one end of the other main length of twisted paper and insert that in the knot, too, then tighten the knot. Working as close to the knot as possible, weave the long paper twist around

the ribs in a circle, going over the first rib next to it, then under the next one, over the next rib, then under again. Keep going around and around, weaving in and out, building up each layer of the basket. Try to keep the layers close and snug and make sure that you don't miss a rib when weaving. When you have only about four inches left of the weaving paper, grab the rib closest to it and twist the two pieces together. Bend them down to the edge of the basket, then grab the next rib and twist that one in. Keep bending the pieces along the rim, twisting in each rib as you go. Tuck the last end and any other loose ends under the rim of the basket, weaving them in on the inside.

7

O! The Joy!

The "high ruged mountains" the Corps crossed are now known as the Bitterroot Range, part of the northern Rocky Mountains. They got their name from the bitterroot (the state flower of Montana), which grows on its rocky ridges. Indians gathered the plant and boiled its carrotlike roots, which made a nutritious if bitter meal. Lewis collected the plant and brought it back to the east. Its scientific name, *Lewisia rediviva*, honors him.

September 1, 1805
The Corps begins crossing the Bitterroot Mountains

The next weeks took every bit of the explorers' strength and determination, for these were the most difficult days of their journey. The men cut trails over the pine-covered hills and inched along, their horses slipping on the steep and rocky slopes. It snowed, then rained. Then sleet, cold and icy, beat down on the men and their horses. Along the way they met a large band of Salish Indians who were on their way east to hunt buffalo. It was a happy meeting. The Indians "threw white robes over our Sholders . . . we Encamped with them and found them friendly," wrote Clark. The captains and their men wondered if these people could be the descendants of the Welsh explorers, for their language sounded unlike that of any other tribe they had met so far. The captains purchased more horses from the Salish, then they set on their way once again.

September 9, 1805
The Corps reaches Travelers' Rest

As the Corps made its way over the mountains, game became more scarce. The men finished the last of their dried meat, their flour, and almost all of their corn. They lived on berries they gathered along the way. After a week of grueling travel they took a day off from their labors and camped near the banks of a mountain stream. Lewis named their campground "Travellers Rest." The stream, their guide Toby told them, connected with a river to the east that flowed into the Missouri River near the distant Gates of the Rocky Mountains. If the captains had known of this route back at those rocky gates, they might have saved weeks of travel and backbreaking work. But they would not have been able to cross the mountains without the horses of the Shoshone, so perhaps they had made the right decision after all.

They spent a day resting and recuperating, and several of the men went out to hunt. One of them, Private Colter, met three Indians who were tracking some horses that had been stolen from them. They were members of a tribe that lived on the far side of the mountains. The captains eagerly asked them about the route ahead. It was encouraging to hear that these mountains could be crossed, because from where the men stood it seemed as if they went on forever.

The next days took the explorers over hills and through deep valleys. One day they came to a hot sulfur spring, its waters boiling out from its source. Shortly after that they crossed a mountain pass. Exhausted by their efforts, the Corps camped that night along a stream in an open glade, surrounded by mountains on all sides. The stream ran to the west. They had crossed the Continental Divide.

Though it was still hot in the plains, here in the mountains, winter had set in. The snow grew deeper every day. Perhaps that made it harder for Toby to follow the path, for he lost his way and led them off the trail. They fought their way back to the path along steep, overgrown, and treacherous ground. On this side of the mountain pass, the slopes were thick with pine and spruce trees, and stands of giant red cedars with branches the size of large trees. The ground was covered with fallen trees, and their path was blocked every way they turned. Their horses slipped and stumbled. When their path took them up another steep ascent, several horses lost their footing altogether and rolled down the steep slopes. Thankfully none of the horses was hurt. Whenever the men climbed a ridge and got a glimpse of the way ahead, they became more discouraged. "High ruged mountains in every direction," wrote Clark.

The supplies of food ran low, then ran out. Finally even the portable soup Lewis had purchased way back in Pennsylvania was gone. The hunters found no deer or other game in the densely forested mountains. Twice, with nothing left to eat, they were driven to kill a horse for a meal. Colt-Killed Creek got its name from this terrible necessity.

The explorers struggled for every mile. Their legs ached with the effort, and their feet were wet and freezing from the ever-deepening snow. Clark wrote that he was as "wet and as cold in every part as I ever was in my life." The men huddled close to huge bonfires at night and listened uneasily to wolves howling in the distance. Late one night the captains decided that the best way to survive this passage over the mountains was to send a party ahead to hunt. Clark and six of the men moved on in advance of the rest of the party, keeping their eyes open for game, for the trail, and for any signs of the Indians who lived west of this mountain range—the Nez Perce.

While Clark moved ahead, Lewis and the rest of the group struggled over ridges and crawled along paths carved out of the sides of steep cliffs. In spite of the difficulties, Lewis managed to make note of the new plants and animals he saw every day. Pheasants avoided the hunters' guns but not Lewis's sharp eyes—he described three different kinds.

One day, with no food left, the Corps made a meal of lard and candles. The next day they were able to catch some birds and small game, but still the men were getting weaker. (Clark's party was not doing much better. Clark named a river "Hungery Creek" because they had nothing to eat the night they camped next to it. Just as it seemed as if they couldn't travel another mile, one of the privates from Clark's hunting party met Lewis's group with good news. Directly ahead, the land leveled into a plain dotted with pine trees. There they would find Clark and the village of the Nez Perce.

September 20, 1805
The Corps meets the Nez Perce

Just the day before, Clark and his companions had met the Nez Perce. Clark had spotted three Indian boys trying to hide in some tall grass. The boys were afraid of the wild-looking white men. Clark assured them of his good intentions by giving them small gifts. The boys led them to their village where the people of the Nez Perce tribe welcomed the strange visitors and fed them dried salmon and roots. Clark approached the chief, Twisted Hair, as he fished in a nearby river. The friendly and cheerful chief welcomed Clark, the first white man he had ever met, and they smiled as they talked with their hands late into the night.

When Lewis arrived, Clark showed him a map that Twisted Hair had drawn for him of the lands to the west. The captains were encouraged by his information. The river next to the Nez Perce village would take them to a larger one, which in turn

Nez Perce girl on horseback

flowed into the Columbia River. Could it be that they would finally arrive at the great Pacific Ocean?

They stayed for two weeks with the Nez Perce while preparing for the next stage of their journey. Nez Perce (Pierced Nose) was the French name for these people, the Chopunnish, who sometimes wore ornamental shells in their pierced noses. This was a village of only 18 lodges, but other bands of the Nez Perce tribe lived in the mountainous country surrounding them. Sometimes the Nez Perce lived in tipis. They also built long A-shaped lodges of poles covered with reeds. The lodges could house many families.

The Nez Perce women made leggings, shirts, dresses, and moccasins from the tanned skins of antelope and deer. Their robes and dresses were ornamented with white beads and seashells. They hung shells from their hair and wore otter skins or braided grasses around their necks. The men wore headbands made of fox or otter fur. Buffalo-hide robes kept them warm in the winter.

In the spring and summer the Nez Perce people camped along the rivers and caught salmon using nets, spears, and special traps. The men hunted for deer and elk. Later in the year the women gathered berries and used sharp sticks to dig for the bulb of the camas plant. They cooked the bulbs in a pit of hot stones or ground them up to make a bread that one of the privates said tasted like pumpkin. Nez Perce hunting parties took their horses to the plains on the other side of the mountains to ride after the buffalo. Berries, salmon, meat, and bulbs were dried and stored for the winter months.

Each season of the year brought its own sacred tradition. In the spring the Nez Perce held a celebration in honor of the salmons' return. In the fall young people were sent on a retreat to fast and ask for a vision. In the winter each person sang his own song and created a dance in honor of his guardian spirit at a special ceremony.

The Corps traded knives and trinkets for dried fish and camas, the plant with the edible bulbs. Following the days of starvation, these new, strange foods made many of the men, including Lewis, very sick. Clark tended to them while the others set to work cutting trees and building dugout canoes. The Nez Perce showed them a new way to hollow out the boats. They set one side of a tree over a low fire until a large cavity was burned in the wood. The men of the Corps made five boats in this fashion. They cached their saddles and some supplies and asked Twisted Hair to keep their horses until their return. Twisted Hair and another chief, Tetoharsky, prepared to join the Corps for a short part of their trip. Finally the Corps was back on a stream, this time going downstream to the west.

This new stream was fast and white with rapids. The explorers raced downstream, their boats flying and crashing over the rocks. One boat was torn by a sharp rock. It quickly filled with water and began to sink. Several of the men couldn't swim; desperately, they hung onto the boat. They managed to bring it to shore and retrieve most of the supplies, but the incident may have frightened their Shoshone guide Toby into leaving—later that night Toby and his son were seen running off into the distance.

Within days, the fast stream took them to a larger river. Canyons rose on either side of this rocky river. Soon the canyons opened into wide plains covered with sagebrush. This place was

Make a Drum

Decorate this drum with pictures and symbols that are special to you!

Materials

- Newspaper
- 10-inch embroidery hoop
- White glue
- ¼ yard of heavy acetate cloth
- Scissors
- Water
- Paper cup
- Paintbrush
- Acrylic paints
- Feathers, ribbons, or other decorative items (such as strings of beads or seashells)

Spread newspaper over your work space. Remove the outer hoop of the embroidery hoop and spread glue around the outside of the inner hoop. Stretch the cloth over the inner hoop. Replace the outer hoop and tighten it. Pull the cloth taut. Let dry for an hour. Trim the extra cloth off with the scissors. Remove the outer hoop.

Mix 3 tablespoons of glue with 1 tablespoon of water in the paper cup. Paint the mixture over the cloth. Let dry for an hour. Add another coat and let dry for another hour.

Paint your own design on the drumhead. Glue feathers to its sides or decorate with other items.

In 1964 archaeologists uncovering a site in eastern Washington found a Jefferson peace medal, one of the medals that Lewis and Clark distributed to Indian chiefs. Other medals are still in the possession of the tribes who received them nearly 200 years ago.

home to many small Indian villages, and the Corps stopped several times to trade for fish and dogs from the tribes. Many of the men felt that the diet of the Nez Perce had made them so sick that they would rather eat dog than roots and fish. Clark also found the diet of roots and dried fish "extremely bad," but he was the only one of the men who was disgusted by eating dog.

The Indians along the river were fascinated by the sight of the Corps of Discovery, this group of men accompanied by a young Indian woman and baby. People came from miles around, on foot and in their canoes, to get a look at the group.

October 16, 1805
The Corps reaches the Columbia River

On the day they came to the Columbia River, the Corps stopped at the junction and made camp. That night a chief led 200 men to their camp, singing and beating on drums as they walked. They formed a circle around the Corps and sang for them. The captains gave them small gifts and presented a medal to the chief.

The Corps camped for two days at this junction. Lewis spent time with the people who visited their camp, members of the Yakima and Wanapam tribes. He took careful notes for a vocabulary of their languages. Many of these Indians practiced a custom that caused people to name them the Flatheads. They would place an infant on a special board and place another board at an angle across the baby's forehead, drawing the second board a little tighter every day until eventually it touched the child's nose. After about a year, the face was

Jefferson peace medal

Salmon

The thousands of salmon Clark saw had just come to the end of a very long journey. Each fish had begun its journey in one of the many creeks and streams that flowed into the Columbia River.

In late winter, tiny salmon (called "alevin") hatch from eggs laid in the rivers' gravel bottoms. A few weeks later, one-inch long and called "fry," they emerge from the gravel to feed and grow until the time comes for their journey downstream. As four-inch "fingerlings" (small fish) they drift downriver and swim out to sea. For the next few years the salmon live in the ocean, traveling thousands of miles and growing as large as 125 pounds and 4 feet in length.

When a salmon reaches maturity, something calls it back to its birthplace. No one quite knows how the salmon sense their way back home. A salmon can be thousands of miles away with several crisscrossing ocean currents between it and its destination, yet when it begins its migration, it travels in the most direct route to the river or creek of its birth. Some scientists think the fish follows its amazing sense of smell—a salmon can smell one drop of a substance in 250 gallons of water! Others believe that the fish navigate by sensing the earth's magnetic fields.

Once the salmon return to the river, they no longer feed. They struggle upstream, swimming through rapids and leaping up 20-foot waterfalls. When they reach their home, the females dig deep nests (called "redds") in the gravel with sweeping motions of their tails, and lay thousands of eggs. The males swim over the eggs and fertilize them. The salmons' lives are now over, and they die within a week. Their bodies provide nutrients that fertilize the soil beneath the stream.

Salmon need cold, clean, oxygen-rich water to thrive and reproduce. The great numbers of salmon that Clark saw have now been reduced by overfishing, logging, and global warming. Dams built along rivers to provide people with electricity make it hard for adult salmon to swim upstream and for the little fingerlings to swim down. Many groups are now working together to find ways to help rebuild the salmon population.

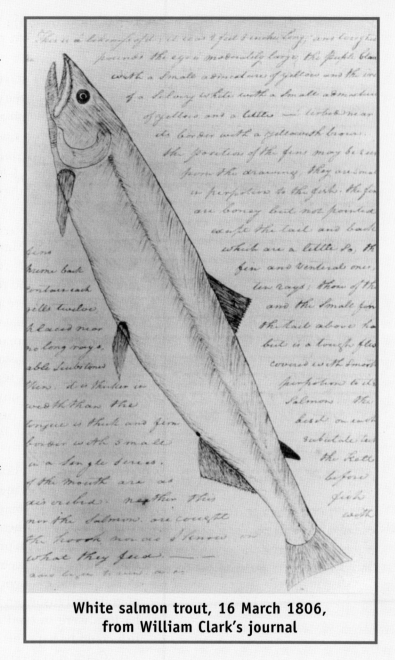

White salmon trout, 16 March 1806, from William Clark's journal

Flathead child

reshaped so that the forehead angled back and formed a straight line from the crown of the head to the tip of the nose.

While Lewis stayed at the camp, Clark took a canoe and two of the men to explore the first few miles of the Columbia River. They passed several islands and saw on each one rectangular lodges and large scaffolds of drying fish. The river held fantastic numbers of salmon. Clark looked down and saw the large fish crowding the river to depths of 15 to 20 feet.

The people who lived along the Columbia River were very busy catching salmon and laying them out to dry. Many, though, were so curious about Clark and his companions that they jumped into their canoes and followed them. Clark stopped at one village where he was treated to a special meal. He sat on a mat and watched as his host prepared salmon. The man heated stones in a fire, then placed them in a basket of water that held a large fish. After the fish was cooked in the simmering water, it was taken out of the basket and placed on a platter made of rushes for Clark's enjoyment. Clark pronounced it delicious and gave a gift of ribbons to his host.

Clark noticed that unlike the men of many of the tribes they had met so far, these men shared in the work of the women. The people lived in long lodges made of rushes and used nets and spears to catch the fish. To preserve the dried fish, they pounded them between two stones until they were thin, then placed them in rectangular baskets made of grass and rushes and lined with salmon skin. The baskets were stacked and covered with mats. The fish could be kept this way for years.

Clark noted especially that these people had great respect for the aged. In one of the lodges Clark visited that day, there was an old woman of "more than 100 winters." Her people had given her the seat of honor, and when the old blind woman spoke, they gave her the greatest respect and attention.

The great chief Yellept, the head of the Walla Walla tribe, honored the captains with a visit. The "bold and handsome" chief brought them a large basket of berries and invited the Corps to stay with his people. The captains gave him a Jefferson medal, and promised to visit the Walla Walla on

Woman and child Flatheads

their return. They were anxious to proceed. The year was drawing to a close, and the Pacific Ocean was only a short distance ahead.

The Columbia River rushed them forward, racing toward the sea. Everywhere, the explorers saw Indians gathering along the banks, marveling at this strange fleet of boats. For a time, their Nez Perce companions, Twisted Hair and Tetoharsky, rode ahead and interpreted for them, but one day the two men returned home. When Clark stopped at one village, the dozens of people who lived there rushed to their lodges, where they cowered in fright. However, when they saw Sacagawea and her baby, they were reassured and came out of their lodges to welcome the group. They had never seen white or black men, but they knew that no war party of any race would travel with a woman and a baby. As the Corps traveled farther down the river, the explorers met Indians who had obviously been in contact with British trading vessels. The captains noted one man wearing a blue sailor's jacket, and others who wore cloth blankets.

The Indians "examined us with much attention," wrote Clark, and treated them kindly, though at times they took small items from the explorers' camp. These people, the Chinook, spoke a language unlike any the explorers had heard. The Chinook built their homes of wood, skillfully paddled the wild river in dugout canoes, decorated themselves with seashells, and practiced the tradition of flattening their heads. Lewis very much wanted one of their beautiful sea-otter robes, but the Indians would not trade one for anything he offered. They only wanted blue beads, and the only beads available were on Sacagawea's beautiful belt. When she saw how much Lewis wanted the robe she gave him

her belt for the trade. Lewis also admired a Chinook canoe and traded a hatchet for it. It was a lovely boat, light and strong, with beautifully carved figures of animals on the bow. The captains traded with the Indians for fish, dried roots, and acorns.

The Corps continued on its journey, flying over whitewater rapids and portaging when the river became too rocky to navigate. When faced with high waterfalls, the explorers lowered their dugouts over the falls with elkskin ropes. One day they came to a place where the wide river narrowed and passed through a small channel between towering black rocks. The wild, rushing waters were "swelling, boiling, and whorling in every direction,"

Canoe with carved images, 1 February 1806, from William Clark's journal

Lewis and Clark on the lower Columbia

wrote Clark. It was a fearful sight, but their great desire to reach the ocean overcame their fears, and they prepared to take their little boats through the narrows. Indians lined up along the top of the rocks to watch them, ready to salvage any supplies that came their way when the boats sank, as they were sure they would. But somehow all five of the dugouts survived the wild and dangerous ride. At a camp beyond the falls, the explorers sang and danced with joy and relief.

The next days brought more danger—the river narrowed and boiled again, then spilled over falls. The little boats bobbed over the rapids. The men strained to carry the supplies over difficult rocky portages and lowered the boats over the largest falls. One day they passed a huge formation they called Beacon Rock, its sheer face rising straight up to a height of 700 feet above the river. Finally, they came to a place where the river widened again.

The land had changed from arid, dry highlands to wet, lush, wooded country. In the mornings the river was covered with a blanket of fog, and on many days the explorers paddled along in relentless rains. Forests of spruce and fir grew along the banks. Harbor seals popped their heads out of the water and looked inquisitively at the passing boats. A condor flew overhead, its broad wings stretching more than nine feet across. Ducks, geese, and cranes flew above in great numbers—once again the birds were traveling south for the winter. Ahead, a mountain showed its snowy peak. Clark recognized it as Mount Hood, which had been discovered by British seamen who had entered the mouth of the Columbia River and ventured a short way upriver.

November 7, 1805
"Ocian in view!" Clark sees land's end in the distance

One day the explorers realized the river was rising and falling in response to the ocean's tides. As they moved forward, the broad river grew even wider and the smell of seawater was in the air. In the distance, they heard the sound of waves crashing. Their goal was just within reach and their spirits rose wildly. "Ocian in view! O! The joy!" Clark wrote in his journal.

But the Corps's joy had to be held in check for a time. The next day they met waves so high that they landed on the north side of the river and drew their dugouts onto the shore. A furious storm was building. Heavy rain dampened their spirits and they were made more uncomfortable by the steep slope they had landed on—there wasn't one level place to sleep on the hilly shore. Soon they were hemmed in by high tide and waves. The Corps was cold and hungry and "every man as wet as water could make them." They were stuck in the uncomfortable camp. Their canoes and baggage drifted on the high waters. Heavy winds and huge waves threw giant tree trunks crashing into their camp. They waited and watched, soaked through, with nothing to eat but dried fish. Sacagawea drew out a little piece of bread she had made from a hoard of flour she had saved for Pomp. She shared it with Clark, who was thrilled to have a mouthful of bread, the first he had tasted in months. It was the only comfort in days of misery. The wind blew and the rain fell.

Things were getting desperate in the watery camp. Clatsop Indians were able to make their way

Good Guesswork

Clark calculated distances by "dead reckoning"—he sighted a landmark ahead and estimated the distance between his location and the landmark. When the boat passed that landmark he chose another. His calculations of the distance they had traveled from the mouth of the Missouri River to the Pacific Ocean were off by only 40 miles.

to the campsite and brought the explorers roots and fish to eat. Clark noted their skill in maneuvering their canoes in the rough waters. Perhaps it encouraged him and Lewis, for they ordered three men to place the Indian canoe in the water and explore along the shoreline to find a better camp. They found an agreeable spot and returned for Captain Lewis and several more of the men.

November 18, 1805
The Corps sees the Pacific Ocean

While Captain Clark organized the rest of the party to move to the new camp, Lewis scouted ahead, eager to stand at the edge of the continent. It must have been an amazing moment when he first saw the vast Pacific Ocean. Lewis celebrated the event by carving his name on a tree at the edge of the shore. The next day, Clark had his turn. With York and several other men, he hiked along the shore and soon stood over the ocean they had worked so hard to reach. Clark, too, carved his name on a tree, "Capt. William Clark December 3d 1805. By Land. U. States in 1804–1805." Later that night he wrote that his men were greatly satisfied with their accomplishments and astonished by the sight of "the high waves dashing against the rocks

and this emence Ocian." They had traveled for 18 months and thousands of miles for this sight.

November 24, 1805
One person, one vote: the Corps votes on where to camp for the winter

The end of the year was at hand and the weather was cold and wet. It was time to build a winter camp. The captains gathered the group together and offered each person the chance to vote on their plans for the winter. They could stay on the north side of the Columbia River, move to the south side and build a winter camp there, or move back inland. Each person, including York and Sacagawea, had a say in the decision and was given a vote. The majority voted for a camp on the south bank. There they could trade with the friendly Clatsop, who told them that elk were available in abundance. The Corps moved across the river, and Captain Lewis traveled ahead to scout for a good site. He found it on a high bluff near a river, close to the ocean and rich with timber and elk.

December 7, 1805
The Corps begins building its winter quarters, Fort Clatsop

The explorers built their home for the winter. The men cut down large trees, and in three weeks of hard labor made a sturdy fort—

Replica of Fort Clatsop

Today, archaeologists are sifting through the soil near the Columbia River, looking for the exact site of Fort Clatsop. Like detectives (only dirtier), they look for clues that will show them where and how the explorers lived. Wooden structures have long ago rotted away, but other clues can point the scientists in the right direction. Archaeologists have found pieces of cloth and an old musket ball that they believe belonged to the Corps of Discovery.

In one of the more unusual efforts, scientists are searching for traces of mercury in the soil. Lewis treated his sick men with pills containing the heavy metal. Mercury passes through the body without breaking down. Traces of mercury in the soil could pinpoint the place where the Corps's outhouse was built! Archaeologists are also hard at work at the campsite below the Great Falls of the Missouri. They've found a number of buffalo bones and features in the soil believed to be impressions made by the expedition's kettles.

Dig It! An Archaeological Activity

Archaeologists look for artifacts (like arrowheads, pieces of pottery, and coins) or other signs of human presence (like fire rings or trenches or impressions showing where walls stood or logs were inserted). They dig and sweep and screen very carefully so they don't miss a thing, and they keep careful records of every inch of the archaeological site. If you find an arrowhead or other signs of an ancient settlement, be sure to let a ranger or other official know. Only licensed archaeologists should excavate a site. Here's an activity for you and one or more friends to practice your archaeological skills.

Materials

- *Sandbox or beach*
- *Lots of small plastic items that you can play with (ask a parent!) such as buttons, bottles, chicken bones, pennies, pieces of cloth, broken utensils*
- *Ruler*
- *Paper*
- *Stakes*
- *String*
- *Pencil*
- *Trowels or old spoons*
- *An old screen*
- *A dustbroom or an old toothbrush*

For this activity one person has to "plant" the archaeological evidence. Maybe a parent will help with this part of the fun. Take the small items to the sandbox or a marked-off area of a beach and bury them at different levels. Cover them with sand and smooth the site over.

Now the archaeologists get to work. Divide the area into small squares (each about 1 foot by 1 foot) by posting stakes one foot apart along all the edges of the sand. Mark the area into squares by stretching string across the sand from post to post. On your paper, draw the area and mark it off into the same number of squares. You will dig within each square and mark on the paper what you find in each. Dig carefully so you don't injure or miss anything. Place the sand on top of the screen and sift it through the screen to catch very small objects. When you find something, write a description of it on your grid.

When you're completely finished with the dig (ask the person who planted the evidence if you have found all the items), sit down with your finds and analyze them. Dust the sand off of the objects with the dustbroom or toothbrush. Pretend they're artifacts from an ancient site. Can you tell what kind of people used these items? Piece together a story from the archaeological evidence and, like a real archaeologist, write a site report on your dig.

a 50-foot, fenced square with a line of three cabins on one side, four cabins on the other, and a parade ground running up the middle. They moved in on Christmas Eve and were quite happy to have a roof between their heads and the constant rain. On Christmas Day the men shouted and shot their muskets and treated their captains to modest gifts they'd purchased from Indians along the river. Sacagawea gave Captain Clark a beautiful string of white weasel tails. The captains gave their men tobacco and handkerchiefs. Even a Christmas dinner of dried fish and spoiled meat did not dampen their spirits.

The Corps named its new home Fort Clatsop in honor of the local tribe. The Clatsop were related to the Chinook who lived along the Columbia River. They were great traders, boaters, and fisherfolk. The Clatsop visited the fort every day, and Lewis made note of their traditions and dress. They wore robes, vests, and skirts of elk and otter skins that they sewed together with cords made from the bark of cedar trees. They also used the bark of the cedar to make mats and blankets. Cone-shaped hats made of cedar bark and bear grass protected them from the constant rain. They wore beaded bracelets and necklaces of elk teeth and seashells. Their tools and utensils, such as bows, arrows, and bowls, were all made of wood. The Clatsop lived in timber homes with cedar bark roofs and carved the giant cedar trees into beautiful canoes that were large enough to hold 20 people and were decorated with elaborate carvings of animals. They hunted elk, seal, deer, and birds, and gathered roots, fruit, seaweed, and shellfish. They caught fish with nets and spears and cooked them in baskets filled with hot stones and water.

The Corps quickly settled into a routine at Fort Clatsop. The explorers posted sentries to keep guard at night. John Shields repaired all the weapons, and the men worked hard to keep them clean of rust in the wet climate. Drouillard hunted for elk and deer. Any meat the explorers didn't eat right away they dried and smoked for later. They cleaned and scraped elkskins for clothing. Everyone made moccasins, until, by the end of the winter, there was a supply of hundreds ready for the return journey. They made repairs to their canoes, gathered berries, and traded with the Indians for dried fish and roots.

It rained all but 12 days during the expedition's four and a half months on the coast. The weather didn't seem to bother the Clatsops, who

Whaling chief's hat

Candlefish

Instead of candles made from elk fat, the Corps could have used the eulachon, or candlefish, for light. These fish, which the Clatsop caught in great quantities, are very fatty. It's said that a wick inserted in a eulachon's body can be lit and burned just like a candlewick.

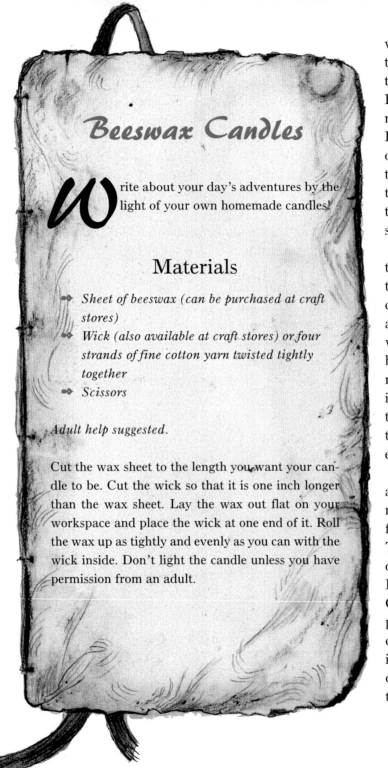

Beeswax Candles

Write about your day's adventures by the light of your own homemade candles!

Materials

- *Sheet of beeswax (can be purchased at craft stores)*
- *Wick (also available at craft stores) or four strands of fine cotton yarn twisted tightly together*
- *Scissors*

Adult help suggested.

Cut the wax sheet to the length you want your candle to be. Cut the wick so that it is one inch longer than the wax sheet. Lay the wax out flat on your workspace and place the wick at one end of it. Roll the wax up as tightly and evenly as you can with the wick inside. Don't light the candle unless you have permission from an adult.

walked cheerfully through the wet forests in their cone-shaped hats, but many members of the Corps fell sick. One of the privates, William Bratton, suffered terribly from back pain. For months he could barely move, and though Lewis tended him in every way he could think of, Bratton's pain didn't lessen. Lewis began to think Bratton might never recover. To make things even worse, fleas invaded every inch of the explorers' clothing. Every day felt the same—wet, dreary, and itchy.

Several of the men felt quite lucky when they were sent to the oceanside for a few weeks to make salt. There they made a comfortable camp near the wooden villages of the Clatsop and the Tillamook. They brought large kettles with them and made huge bonfires on the beach. They kept the fires burning day and night and boiled the sea water down until nothing remained but fine, white salt. They packed the salt into large kegs and brought it back to the fort, where it was a welcome addition to the explorers' diet.

The men returning from the oceanside also brought with them some blubber they'd received from the Indians, who had taken it from a whale that had washed up on the coast. They ate it and found the tender meat a wonderful change from their daily diet of tough elk. Lewis said the blubber was not unlike beaver. Clark was determined to get more and prepared to set out with a small group for the coast. When Sacagawea heard of this plan, she insisted on going. She had not yet seen the ocean and was not about to be left behind this time. Lewis wrote that she told the captains

The Sea Otter

Sea otters are the sea-dwelling relatives of river otters, weasels, minks, and skunks. These playful animals are perfectly adapted to their life at sea, with broad, webbed back feet that act as flippers and dense fur to keep them warm in the cold waters of the ocean. Male sea otters can grow to 5 feet long and 80 pounds; the females are slightly smaller. A sea otter has a long body and short legs, dark brown fur on its back and belly, a white head and white whiskers, and big black eyes. Groups, or "rafts," of sea otters float on their backs in beds of "kelp" (seaweed) when they aren't diving deep underwater to gather shellfish and sea urchins for dinner.

Shellfish, such as mussels and abalone, present a certain problem for the diner—how to crack open the shells. The sea otter's solution is to choose a stone, place it on its chest, and pound the shell against the stone with its paws, all while floating on its back.

After a delicious seafood dinner, the otter carefully cleans its fur, blowing air into it to help itself stay afloat. Baby sea otter "pups" sometimes need a little extra help in the water. When the mother needs to hunt, she wraps her baby in a piece of kelp to keep it afloat. Sea otters have just one pup at a time and keep it close by for more than a year to teach it how to dive and hunt for food.

The sea otter population along the Pacific coast dropped from an estimated 20,000 animals to only 50. With protection, the numbers increased for a time, but the sea otter population is again in decline.

"She had traveled a long way with us to see the great waters and that now that monstrous fish was also to be seen, she thought it very hard she could not be permitted to see either." She got her way. It was the least they could do for the Indian woman who had proved so helpful to them on their journey.

Sacagawea finally saw the great ocean. There was not much left to see of the giant whale. By the time the group arrived the Indians had stripped it of its blubber so that only a large skeleton, over 100 feet long, remained. The Indians were already busily boiling down some of the blubber into oil. Clark coaxed them into selling him several hundred pounds of the blubber and a few gallons of the precious oil.

Clark was surprised to hear many English words from these people who lived on the coast. They'd been in contact with British and American traders who sailed their ships to the Pacific coast to trade blankets and tools for elk and otter skins. The captains would have been very glad to see one of these trading vessels. They were hungry for news from home, they had few supplies, and they'd hoped to send word back to President Jefferson through a ship's captain that they had reached their goal. Strangely, a Boston ship, the *Lydia*, arrived on the shores during their stay along the Pacific coast, but the expedition never saw or got word of the ship's presence.

The blubber and oil didn't last long. Drouillard had to hike farther every day to find elk to feed the hungry Corps. They were running out of goods to trade for roots and fish. They ran out of candles but fortunately had brought molds and wicks. Lewis set the men to work making candles from elk fat.

At night, by the candle's light, Captain Lewis wrote detailed descriptions of the many animals and plants he had encountered over the previous months. He described the magnificent Sitka spruce and "the next in dignity," the mountain hemlock. He collected and labeled leaves, plants, and cones. He described dozens of animals, some of which (such as the elk that is native to this region) had never before been seen by white people. He devoted one entry to the sea otter. He described the animal's deep, thick, glossy fur, small ears and eyes, and webbed feet. He included the Indian names for the adult otter (e-luck-ke) and the infant otter (spuck).

Captain Clark spent painstaking hours perfecting his map of the journey from Fort Mandan to the site on the Pacific coast. As he plotted the twists and turns of the Missouri River and the other rivers they had followed to the west, he and Captain Lewis discussed their return. They decided that on the way east they would investigate other routes. They would split up the party when they reached Travelers' Rest, their campsite in the mountains. From there Lewis would travel with one group to the Great Falls of the Missouri, then explore Maria's River. Clark would take the rest of the party along a route to the south of Lewis's. They would travel to the Three Forks of the Missouri, then follow the Yellowstone River until it joined the Missouri River. There the two groups would reunite.

8

Our Homeward Bound Journey

During the long, cold months it seemed as if the time for departure would never come. But eventually spring arrived, and everyone eagerly turned to preparing for the return journey. The Corps repaired and packed the dugouts. On the morning they planned to depart, March 23, the weather was rainy and windy, but by afternoon the sun had come out and the Corps began its journey. The explorers placed their canoes in the wide waters of the Columbia River and turned their heads and hearts toward home.

The Corps hadn't traveled far when it met a band of Chinook Indians paddling downriver. The news the Chinook told them was discouraging—the salmon had not yet begun their upstream journey. The people who lived along the river were very hungry. The captains, concerned about supplies, ordered their men to make camp. They spent several days hunting and drying meat for their journey. Game was scarce between here and the Nez Perce villages, and without the salmon there would be hungry days ahead.

It was a struggle to bring their boats up the rough waters of the Columbia River. Violent winds tossed the canoes. The waves were so high the explorers had to wait on land for the waters to calm. It rained constantly, and at night flood tides swamped their camps. But slowly the Corps made headway. They measured their progress against the snow-covered peaks of Mount Hood and Mount Saint Helens on either side of the river.

The Corps passed Beacon Rock and arrived at the base of the rapids once again. Lewis made camp with several of the men, including Private Bratton, who was still in great pain and could barely walk. The rest pulled and carried the canoes over the rapids one at a time. It took all of their strength to keep the boats from crashing against the huge rocks. The portage was long and dangerous, the rocky trail slippery with rain. The men at the camp were constantly on their guard against the local Indians, who crowded into their camp in large numbers. Lewis called them "scoundrels" because they took eating utensils, knives, tomahawks, a saddle and a robe, and even made off with Lewis's dog Seaman. This made Lewis terribly angry, and he sent three men after them to demand the surrender of his dog. When the Indians saw the armed men coming after them, they let Seaman go and ran for their lives.

The captains were eager to leave the river behind and travel overland to the lands of the Nez Perce tribe. Lewis took over the work of the portage and Clark visited a village to trade for horses. After some hard bargaining Clark had enough horses to carry their supplies and the ailing Private Bratton.

While Clark was trading for horses, the salmon appeared in the river. There was great rejoicing among the Chinook. They took the first fish they caught and divided it among all the children in their village. This ritual, noted Clark, was done in the belief that it would hasten the appearance of the rest of the salmon.

With great relief the explorers left the river behind, loaded the horses, and walked. The days were hot, the nights were cold, and after a few days of walking on the rocky land, everyone's feet were very sore. Within a week they arrived at the village of the Walla Walla chief Yellept, who welcomed them with an armload of firewood and a hearty meal of fish. He honored Clark with the gift of a beautiful white horse and made the captains feel so welcome that they spent three days at his village. One night Yellept held a special celebration and hundreds of people from nearby villages came to see the strange visitors. Cruzatte played his fiddle and everyone danced. When the time came to leave these welcoming people, the explorers were rested and happy, and they had additional horses and directions for a shortcut to the Nez Perce villages.

May 11, 1806
The Corps reunites with the Nez Perce

As they continued their journey, the explorers were very pleased to run into their Nez Perce guide, Chief Tetoharsky. He conducted them over rocky hills to the village of their other Nez Perce friend, Twisted Hair, who had agreed to keep their horses over the previous winter. The captains were anxious to find him and their horses so they could once again cross the forbidding mountains ahead of them.

The Corps passed through a number of Indian encampments, where the explorers traded from their meager supply for dried roots and dogs. Since their stay with the Nez Perce the previous fall, Clark's reputation among the Indians had spread from village to village. He had doctored two men, one for a painful knee and the other for a growth on his thigh. Both had happily recovered and praised the red-headed captain's great medicine. When Clark reappeared, many people lined up to receive medical treatment from him, and he was able to trade his skills for food. Even so, it was hard to find enough food to feed all of the explorers. When they reached the lodge of a great chief, Broken Arm, the captains told him that their supplies were low. They asked if they could trade one of their thin horses for a fat colt to eat. Broken Arm wouldn't hear of a trade, and instead gave them two horses.

The explorers were impatient to move on, but their journey came to a standstill at Broken Arm's village. The snow was too deep in the mountains ahead. They held a council in the great chief's lodge, and all the chiefs of the nearby villages came to listen to Lewis's speech. He called on them to make peace with the Blackfoot on the other side of the mountains. Supplied with guns from French traders to the north and rich with horses, the powerful Blackfoot dominated the neighboring tribes. The Nez Perce chiefs, in turn, counseled the captains to put off their journey and to stay with them until the snow melted. Chief Twisted Hair collected the Corps's scattered horses and their journey was delayed for almost a month.

Every day the captains looked anxiously at the white mountains. It was warm in their

A Blackfoot chief

Lewis described Mount Saint Helens as "the most noble-looking object of its kind in nature." The mountain has changed its shape since the Corps of Discovery passed it. The Indians knew that it was an active volcano. They called it "louwala-clough" (smoking mountain). British sea captain George Vancouver named it Mount Saint Helens in 1792.

Tranquil when the Corps of Discovery passed it, the mountain erupted several times in the 1800s. On May 18, 1980, it exploded. A huge earthquake rocked the land, followed by a nine-hour eruption that burned down forests, choked streams, and changed the entire appearance of the mountain. Molten ash and rock heated to 1,500 degrees surged down the mountain's sides at 100 miles an hour. Over 450 tons of ash blew 15 miles into the sky and covered 11 nearby states. The 200 square miles immediately surrounding the mountain were devastated. Today, scientists study the changing landscape around Mount Saint Helens and watch the progress of plants and animals as they reappear on the mountain's slopes.

camp, but they knew from experience that in the mountains winter still held its grip. Clark wrote that he could witness summer, spring, and winter in the "short space of twenty or thirty miles." The captains checked the waters of the nearby river to see if they were rising with melted snow. Clark kept very busy treating his Indian patients, who now lined up for him every morning. They paid him in food and horses.

Though Clark had great success with his Indian patients, neither captain had been able to help Private Bratton. He couldn't walk and could barely sit. One day Private Shields suggested they try the traditional Indian sweatlodge to treat Bratton. The captains agreed that it was worth a try and set Shields to work on building one.

Shields dug a deep hole, placed rocks in the bottom, and built a large fire over them. He then put out the fire and placed a seat over the heated rocks. Several men lowered Bratton onto the seat. Willow poles were bent to form an awning over his head, and blankets were placed on top of them. Bratton was given some water that he sprinkled on the heated rocks to create steam, and he stayed in the sweat lodge until he could barely breathe. When he couldn't bear it any more, they took him out and plunged him in ice-cold water, then returned him to the lodge for another sweat. The next day Bratton walked, free from pain for the first time in months.

When an Indian patient who couldn't move came to Clark, Clark thought of the sweat lodge. The patient, a chief, was carried to Clark on a robe. This man had been unable to move his arms or legs for several years. The chief was lowered into a sweat lodge. After several treatments over the course of a few days, he was able to wiggle his fingers and his toes, then, to his great joy, he was once again able to move his arms and legs.

Pomp, too, became very sick. Both captains wrote in their journals of their concern for the 15-month-old toddler. The cheerful little boy, usually smiling and dancing on his fat, sturdy legs, was limp and feverish, and his throat was swollen and red. The captains treated him by placing salves of bear oil, beeswax, and wild onion on his throat. They were relieved and happy when he recovered from his illness.

Though busy with his patients, Clark still had time to observe the ways of the Nez Perce people. When Private Collins came to camp with two bears he had killed, Clark noted the method the Indians used to steam the meat over a fire. Collins gave the bears' claws to one of the chiefs, for the Nez Perce considered the bear to be a creature of great power. The Indians eagerly ate the meat, and so did the members of the Corps. They were glad to have the roots and wild onions gathered by Sacagawea, too.

The Corps's supply of trading materials was very low. Soon, all they had left was a little vermilion dye, a few needles and thread, and some ribbon. The men even cut the buttons from their coats to trade with the Indians for roots, fish, and camas bread. The hunters walked far and wide to bring game in to the camp.

One day one of the hunters brought Lewis a woodpecker with a black back, a red face, and a white collar. Lewis described it at length in his journal. He also wrote about a beautiful little bird with a bright yellow body and a red head—the western tanager. Wildflowers were in bloom, and Lewis collected and described many plants, 10 of them new to science.

The men of the Corps kept busy, too, but life wasn't all hunting and chores. "In the evening," Clark wrote, "several foot races were run by the men of our party and the Indians; after which our party devided and played at prisoners base untill night. After dark the fiddle was played and the party amused themselves in danceing." Foot and horse races were favorite pastimes of the Nez Perce, and the men of the Corps happily joined them. They also held shooting matches. Games of Prisoner's Base went on for hours—opposing teams took prisoner anyone who was caught away from his team's safe home base.

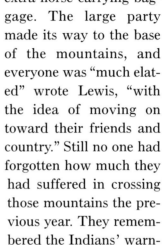

Blackfoot chasing buffalo

Still, everyone in the entire Corps was eager to continue the journey. Back at Fort Clatsop, Lewis had written longingly of that day in the future when he would once again be with his friends in the United States. Clark now looked anxiously at the mountains in front of him and described them as "that icy barier which seperates me from my friends and Country." It had been two years since they set out from their camp near St. Louis. It was a long time to be away. Did their family and friends even remember them?

Every day the captains asked their Nez Perce friends about the route ahead. The Indians advised them to wait—the mountains were still not safe to cross. But their desire to move on was too great, and the explorers began preparations for the mountain crossing. They gathered their saddles and packed supplies of camas roots and bread. The Indians held a big good-bye party for them, with food, games, and dancing. The Corps left the Nez Perce village and headed toward the mountains.

Between the horses they had left with Twisted Hair and those they had traded for, the Corps now had enough so that everyone could ride and lead an extra horse carrying baggage. The large party made its way to the base of the mountains, and everyone was "much elated" wrote Lewis, "with the idea of moving on toward their friends and country." Still no one had forgotten how much they had suffered in crossing those mountains the previous year. They remembered the Indians' warnings—wait another moon, they had said, or there will be no grass on the mountains for the horses to eat. Here at the base of the mountains it was hard to believe that the crossing would be difficult. There was plenty of grass, and the hills and valleys were thick with wildflowers in bloom. The blue flowers of the camas plant were so plentiful that Lewis mistook them for a lake covering the land.

Lewis noted another sign of spring as they rode up the trail—a tiny nest and its maker, a broad-tailed hummingbird. The little bird, with its shiny green back and brilliant red throat, looked like a big insect. Its rapid wingbeats (80 per second) made a humming sound that gave it its name.

Namesakes

In Lewis's honor, the black woodpecker he described at the camp near the Nez Perce village is called Lewis's Woodpecker. Clark's name was given to a beautiful gray, white, and black bird he saw in the mountains—Clark's Nutcracker. Two towns are also named in the captains' honor—Lewiston, Idaho, and Clarkston, Washington.

Trail Signs

Native Americans used different signs to mark trails. They piled up stones to point the way and made slashes on trees—high up the trunks so they wouldn't be covered by snow.

Materials

- *Paper and pencil*
- *Stones*
- *Twigs and branches*
- *Acorns*
- *Chalk*

Make a map of your neighborhood and plot out a path for your friends to follow. Go out on the path yourself and place trail signs for them to use as clues pointing the way. Send your friends out on the trail and see who can find their way to the end first. Here are some trail signs you can use on your path:

- Pile two stones on top of each other. Place a third stone next to the pile in the direction you want your friends to follow.

- Two long twigs laid side by side can mean "follow this path."

- A number of twigs stuck in the ground can indicate distance. Plant 10 twigs side by side to say "10 giant steps."

- When you want your friends to turn a corner, point a bent branch in the direction you want them to take.

- To indicate something hidden (a cache) make a little pile of acorns.

- Twigs placed in the shape of a tipi can mean "go back to home base."

- Danger! Draw a modified bear print—a circle with five claws—in the dirt with a stick or on the sidewalk with chalk.

- When Indians left a broken arrow across a trail it meant "don't go any farther." You can use two crossed branches in the shape of an X to say the same thing.

Make up your own signals, too, and send your friends off on the hunt!

The trail took the Corps up steep slopes, through thick woods, and over downed trees. As they progressed up the mountains, the explorers began to see snow. It grew deeper and deeper until soon the horses were walking on hard-packed drifts eight to ten feet deep. Though they could travel over the top of the snow, it was hard for them to keep to the trail. Eventually the explorers recognized Hungry Creek, where Clark's party had gone to bed hungry the previous September. Here, they camped for the night.

The next day the Corps realized that the Indians were right. The snow got deeper as they climbed until eventually it was 15 feet deep. Whole trees were covered! They found no grassy patches to feed their horses, and they kept losing the trail in the snow. Cold, wet, and discouraged, they decided to turn back. They built a platform for their extra supplies and left them there to pick up on their next try. On their retreat, Private Potts accidentally cut his leg with a knife; Private Colter's horse rolled off the trail and down a rocky slope.

June 10, 1806
The Corps sets off to cross the Bitterroot Mountains

A little over a week later the Corps tried again. This time they had several Nez Perce guides who agreed to show them the way over the mountains. The extra time made a big difference. When they reached the platform holding their supplies, they noticed that the snow had melted many feet. Still, the drifts were deep and grass was hard to find. The young Indians knew exactly where to go, however, to find places where the sun had melted the snow. By the end of each day they led the Corps to camps where their horses could graze.

Along the trail one day the explorers came across a large mound of stones piled eight feet high, with a long pine pole jutting out from the top. It was a sign placed there by Indians to mark the trail. They stopped here and looked around at the view of steep and frightening mountains and were grateful for those "most admireable pilots," their Nez Perce guides.

July 4, 1806
Back at Travelers' Rest, the Corps separates into smaller parties

Over the next few days the Corps retraced their terrible journey of the previous year. They camped one night near the hot sulfur spring. The explorers lowered their stiff, exhausted bodies into the steaming waters. Finally, they reached Travelers' Rest. Here was where the party would split up. They stopped to rest and prepare.

Though it was more dangerous to travel in smaller parties, the captains wanted to explore several routes. Lewis wanted to find the shorter route to the Great Falls of the Missouri that the guide Toby had told them about. He also wanted to explore the river he had named after his cousin Maria. (According to the terms of the Louisiana Purchase, the United States held all the lands watered by the tributaries of the Missouri River, including Maria's River. By finding its northernmost point, Lewis could determine his country's northern boundary.) With another group, Clark

Hummingbirds weigh just ounces and are only a few inches long, but they are fearless. An angry hummingbird will even try to scare off a hawk if it's near the little bird's nest. Hummingbirds migrate hundreds of miles and fly up to 30 miles per hour. They drink nectar from flowers with their long bills, and because they use up so much energy they eat every 15 minutes. They have a unique wing structure that allows them to fly backward, sideways, and up and down. The male performs amazing aerial acrobatics to show off for his mate, looping and diving in the air. The female hummingbird tends to the nest and feeds the young, which hatch from tiny eggs the size of peas.

expressed concern about Lewis's plans, for they were sure his group would meet with trouble. Lewis's path would take him and his men into the country of the Blackfoot tribes.

Lewis was worried, too. He wrote in his journal that "I took leave of my worthy friend and companion Capt. Clark and the party that accompanyed him. I could not avoid feeling much concern on this occasion although I hoped this separation was only momentary." The Nez Perce guides led Lewis and his group of nine men, including Drouillard and the brothers, Reuben and Joseph Field, down the trail.

When they reached the banks of a white and rapid river, the Indians quickly made deerskin pouches for their baggage and swam their horses across the river. Lewis's horses swam, too, and his men followed on hastily-made timber rafts. At camp that night the Indians told Lewis how to follow the trail ahead. He should head in the direction of the waters they called the River of the Road to the Buffalo. From there, the trail was plain to the falls of the Missouri. The Indians were sad to leave their new friends, and Lewis expressed sorrow at the parting, too. The Nez Perce had shown them many kindnesses. Lewis directed his hunters to provide their guides with a supply of deer meat, and he gave them small gifts of clothing and ammunition. In the morning the Indians turned back, and Lewis and his men set off to the east.

Lewis's party left the mountains and the evergreen forests. Wide views opened up before them. Ahead were rough, broken plains intersected by streams shining in the bright summer sun. Lewis came upon a clear and pretty creek he named for his favorite member of the expedition—Seaman.

would explore the Yellowstone River. The two groups planned to meet again at the fork of the Yellowstone and Missouri Rivers.

On the Fourth of July they set off to travel their separate paths. The Nez Perce guides had agreed to lead Lewis for one day to be sure he was on the right path. After that, they said, they would leave to find their friends, a Flathead tribe that camped nearby. They didn't want to run into enemy warriors in the lands ahead. The guides

Once again they were in buffalo country. The great beasts were everywhere, gathering in huge herds for their mating season. The males bellowed and fought, and their constant roaring kept the men up at night. They saw elk and deer, signs of bear and wolves, and the tracks of horses—a sign that Indians were nearby.

In just over a week they reached White Bear Island, their old camp at the base of the Great Falls. Lewis tried to count the huge numbers of buffalo. He estimated that there were no less than 10,000 of them within two miles. But that seemed like nothing compared to the number of mosquitoes in their camp! They could barely open their mouths without swallowing a few. Seaman howled, Lewis wrote, "with the torture he experiences from them."

The explorers killed several buffalo to eat and used their skins to make two boats. They crossed the river to their old camp and dug up the cache they had left at this site. High river water had damaged many of the items. Lewis's collection of plants was destroyed. His cache of medicines was "past recovery." But the wheels they had carved from the cottonwood trees to portage their boats were still intact, and Clark's maps of the Missouri River had escaped damage.

One morning the explorers woke to find that seven of their horses were gone. Perhaps they'd wandered off, Lewis thought. He sent some of the men out to track them while others busied themselves hunting and drying meat. When Drouillard didn't return from tracking the horses, Lewis worried that he'd had a brush with a grizzly bear. Drouillard returned the next day. He had found horse tracks, along with signs of a recent Indian camp. It seemed as if their horses had been stolen.

Another man, Private Hugh McNeal, did have a brush with a bear. While he was scouting, a grizzly bear frightened his horse. The horse threw him and bolted, and McNeal fell on the ground right beneath the bear! The fierce animal reared up. Just as the bear was about to attack, McNeal scrambled to his feet and struck it on the head with his musket, which broke in two. The bear sat down and scratched his head. McNeal ran for the nearest tree and climbed to its highest branches. There he perched while the bear paced the ground beneath him. Finally, after several suspenseful hours, the animal became bored and lumbered away.

The next day Lewis set out with Drouillard and the Field brothers to explore Maria's River. The others stayed behind to wait for a group from Captain Clark's party to help them portage past the Great Falls. Lewis and his three men must have felt very lonely as they rode their horses across the open country. Lewis said it was like the wide ocean, with "not a tree or shrub to be seen." They felt exposed; such a small party was easy prey for grizzly bears or hostile Indians.

Two days and two river crossings took them to Maria's River. They crossed and followed it upstream. Lewis described its red and yellow clay bluffs and the trees that hugged its banks. At night the four men camped along the stony shores under the rustling branches. After several days of travel to the north and west, Lewis called a halt to their mission. He could see that the river's source was in the mountains to the distant west and that its course had turned. They had reached the northernmost point. The men made camp, and Lewis hoped that the gray skies would clear so he could measure their latitude before returning to the Missouri River.

They stayed at their camp for several cloudy days, Lewis impatiently wishing for clear skies so he could use his instruments. While they waited, Drouillard scouted and discovered a recently abandoned Indian camp. They had received good treatment at the villages of so many tribes, but they'd been warned to fear the Blackfoot. Lewis felt they were "extreemly fortunate in not having met with these people." They weren't so lucky in their attempts to determine their latitude, however, and Lewis named this northernmost encampment Camp Disappointment. They prepared to leave.

July 27, 1806
Lewis and his men fight
with the Blackfoot

The men hadn't traveled far when they saw eight young Indian men and a herd of horses on a rise in the land before them. They were too close to risk fleeing; if the Indians spotted them running it would only show weakness. Instead, Lewis and his men advanced toward the group, with Joseph Field holding a flag high. As they approached, one of the Indians galloped toward them full speed, threatening to "count coup" on the strangers. Lewis and his men stood their ground; the Indian stopped short. Then Lewis rode forward alone and shook hands with the young men. The Indians were Piegan (also called "Pikuni," meaning "Poorly Dressed Ones"), who together with the Blood (known as "Kainah," or "Many Chiefs") and the Blackfoot (or "Siksika," for their dark moccasins) were members of the Blackfoot Confederacy. One of the earliest plains tribes, the Blackfoot now lived in the foothills of the mountains northwest of the Great Plains. Like other plains tribes, their lives revolved around the buffalo. They didn't stay in permanent villages but lived in traveling camps in tipis. The Blackfoot became dominant when they acquired horses, which allowed them to migrate with the herds. They were excellent riders and hunters, and brave and fierce warriors. For battle the warriors painted their horses just as they painted their own faces and bodies. Some even had their horses buried with them when they died.

Lewis indicated that his party was friendly. He gave the Indians small gifts to show his good intentions. The groups moved together to a comfortable camp along the river and built shelter for the night. With Drouillard signing, Lewis learned that a large Piegan camp was close by and that the people had a steady trade with fur traders from the north who brought them guns. The Piegan learned that there were more of these white strangers in their land, who had been in contact with many other tribes, some of whom were their enemies. Both parties had reasons to become fearful and tense as they exchanged information. But for the moment all seemed well, and they settled down for the night. Lewis and his men took turns keeping watch.

Private Joseph Field's watch was the last one of the night. As the sun came up, he set his rifle down for a moment—a terrible mistake. One of the young Piegan saw his chance, grabbed Field's and his brother Reuben's guns, and ran off. Another warrior grabbed Lewis's rifle, and a third grabbed Drouillard's. The rest of the Indians jumped up and herded the white men's horses away from the camp. Lewis quickly grabbed his pistol and ran after the man who had taken his gun, warning him to lay down the rifle. He did so and slowly walked away. Drouillard retrieved his from one of the other Piegans. The Field brothers chased the third, caught him, and threw him to the ground. During the fight Reuben pulled out a knife, and within minutes the Piegan man was dead.

The explorers then turned to chasing the men who were herding the horses away. Lewis ran after one group by himself. As he caught up, he saw that one of them held a musket. As the man turned toward Lewis, Lewis fired his gun. His shot killed the man, but not before he had a chance to fire one shot at Lewis. The bullet barely missed him—Lewis felt the wind of the bullet as it passed his head. The Field brothers chased the others, who escaped with some of the horses. Lewis and his men met back at the camp and hastily saddled their horses for an escape.

Two men were dead, a tragic incident in the Corps of Discovery's otherwise peaceful passage through the land. There was no time to ponder over the events right now, though—the Piegan would certainly try to take revenge for the killings. Lewis, Drouillard, and the Field brothers jumped onto their horses and urged them forward. They rode all that day and late into the stormy night, their way lit by the moon and the bright flashes of lightning bolts. They rode for 100 miles, took a short rest, then mounted again. As they neared the Missouri River, they heard gunshots—not those of vengeful Piegan, but of hunters from the Corps who were camped along the river.

With great relief, Lewis and the men rejoined their companions—the three men they had left at the Falls along with 10 of the men from Clark's party. These men, led by Sergeant Ordway, had

traveled with Captain Clark from Travelers' Rest to the place where they had cached their canoes before crossing the mountains. Clark had then instructed Ordway to take a crew downriver in the canoes to assist Lewis's men in portaging past the Great Falls. They had completed that difficult portage and were waiting for Lewis along the Missouri River with one pirogue and five canoes. Now they placed all their equipment in the boats and set off downstream as quickly as they could travel.

Captain Clark's party, reduced to 10 men, Sacagawea, and little Pomp, had parted from the rest of the group at the Three Forks of the Missouri River to explore the region of the Yellowstone River. This was Sacagawea's country, and when

Blackfoot on horseback

Bighorn Sheep

Able to leap deep chasms in a single bound, bighorns are the superheroes of the sheep world. They make their homes in remote mountains and perch on seemingly sheer cliff faces. Single lambs (and occasional twins) are born on the most out-of-the-way ridges their mothers can find. Within a day or two, a lamb can climb nearly as well as its mother. A week later they rejoin their small herd.

Bighorn sheep see very well and make breath-taking leaps and climbs to avoid cougars, wolves, and humans. They live on grasses, shrubs, and buds of trees. In the winter they paw through the snow to get to their food. Their mating season is in the fall, when small herds gather into larger ones of 100 sheep or more. The males ("rams"), which have magnificent, tightly curved horns, square off for battle. Dueling rams walk away from each other, turn, then rear up on their hind legs and charge forward. At the last moment they drop down onto all fours and crash their massive horns together. Dazed, they back up and do it again, fighting for hours until one of them cries the bighorn version of "uncle."

she pointed the way through a gap in the mountains Clark listened to her advice. The party moved its 50 horses east toward the Yellowstone River.

They crossed open, rocky plains and waded across streams crowded with beaver. Elk and antelope looked up as they passed, then returned to their grazing. Clark prodded his horse into a gallop to chase a grizzly bear. His horse's feet were so sore from traveling over the stony ground that the horse couldn't catch up with the swift grizzly. That night, the men made buffalo skin moccasins for the horses to give them some relief.

One day the explorers saw smoke rising into a cloudless sky. It seemed obvious that this was a signal, but Clark didn't know what it could mean. Perhaps they were smoke signals sent by the Crow Indians. The Crow people (also called "Absaroke")—not-so-distant relatives of the Hidatsa tribes along the Missouri River—made their home here near the Yellowstone River. Had they spotted Clark's party from afar? The next day Charbonneau saw someone standing against the distant horizon.

When the explorers reached the Yellowstone River, they made camp for several days while the men cut down two large trees to make dugout canoes. The next morning, though they hadn't heard a thing during the night, they woke up to find that half of their horses were gone. A scouting mission didn't uncover one trace of the horses' tracks—it was as if the horses had just disappeared! But when one of the men found a moccasin, Clark

Stone walls on the upper Missouri

suspected that their horses had been stolen by the Crow. They seemed to be having a string of bad luck. Charbonneau had been thrown by his horse and hurt. Private George Gibson had snagged his thigh, cutting himself so badly that he could barely walk (Clark named the spot where this accident occurred "Thigh Snagged Creek"). Wolves had stolen into the explorers' camp and eaten their supply of dried meat. They were glad to have some time to recover.

When the canoes were finished, Clark gave instructions for the rest of the journey back to the Missouri River. He ordered Sergeant Pryor and three privates to take the remaining horses overland to the Mandan villages. Clark, with seven men, Sacagawea and Pomp, lashed the two canoes together and set off down the Yellowstone River. The river, high from spring snowmelt, took them swiftly downstream past the yellow banks that had given the Yellowstone its name.

One day the explorers had to pull ashore and wait for an hour as a herd of buffalo swam across the river. The huge beasts pushed their way through the current with chests heaving. As they pulled themselves up the river's bank, water poured off their coarse brown hides. On another day the explorers passed a sandbar and surprised a huge grizzly bear fishing there. It rose on its hind legs then jumped in the water after them. Clark shot his musket to frighten it off. They saw dozens of bighorn sheep looking down on them from high cliffs. Clark hiked up the Bighorn River; he named a creek flowing into it after York.

July 25, 1806
Clark carves his name on
Pompey's Tower

Clark's party floated past a yellow sandstone formation, 200 feet high, its broken and rocky face towering over the river. Clark had the party stop, and he climbed the tall rock to get a view of the country around them. To the west he saw the snow-covered mountains they'd left behind, to the east the winding river that would take them home. Two tall piles of stones on the top of the formation and pictures of animals carved on the cliff face showed him that he was not the first to have made the difficult climb. Clark couldn't resist the temptation to make his mark here, too, and he carved "Wm. Clark July 25, 1806" on the cliff's face. He named the towering formation for Jean Baptiste "Pomp" Charbonneau—the rock was christened Pompey's Tower.

The river rushed the explorers downstream. In one day they traveled 80 miles, and in a little over a week they reached the junction of the Yellowstone and Missouri Rivers. On their journey west when they had come to this place, the Corps had celebrated with a feast and a song. This time Clark's small party looked around and hoped that their companions were safe and would soon join them again. There was no sign of Captain Lewis and his men.

They tried to make camp at the meeting place, but there was no game to be found, and the mosquitoes were so thick that they made life unbearable. Clark decided to take his group farther downstream. He wrote a note for Captain Lewis and left it on a pole at the fork of the rivers.

Prehistoric pictographs

121

Days later, at their camp downstream, Clark's party was joined not by Lewis, but by Sergeant Pryor and the three privates. The four men had set off to bring horses to the Mandan villages, but one night all of their horses were stolen! They had followed the tracks of the animals, but it had soon become clear that they would never catch up. The men had made their way to the river, killed a buffalo, and built two bullboats. Then they had hurried downstream to catch up with Clark's party.

The next day there was still no sign of Lewis, but the explorers were surprised by a party coming from the other direction. Two fur traders came paddling toward them upstream. They introduced themselves as Joseph Dickson and Forest Hancock. They were on a trapping expedition, hoping to make their fortune in the wilderness. The sight of these white strangers was very odd after the long months in the west. The newcomers had been hunting and trapping for a year and had spent the winter with the Teton Sioux. They had seen the keelboat, the *Discovery*, coming down the Missouri as it made its way back to St. Louis.

August 12, 1806
Lewis and Clark reunite at the junction of the Missouri and Yellowstone Rivers

At last, after more than a month apart, Clark saw the boats of his companions coming downstream. But his relief quickly gave way to alarm when he realized that Lewis was lying down in the pirogue. Something must be terribly wrong!

Something was wrong, but nothing that time wouldn't heal. Lewis had made the big mistake of going hunting with Pierre Cruzatte, who was blind in one eye and nearsighted in the other. They were following a herd of elk along the river. Lewis killed one and Cruzatte wounded another, then they reloaded their guns and took different paths after the wounded animal. Just as Lewis was about to fire on the elk, he felt a terrific pain in his "hinder" parts. Cruzatte had shot Lewis, mistaking his buckskin-clad captain for an elk! He tried to deny his mistake, but there wasn't anyone else nearby to blame. It was lucky that the wound wasn't any worse, but it did take Lewis weeks to recover. Still, the Corps was reunited and everyone was happy to be together again.

9

What Marvels We Found

August 14, 1806
The Corps returns to the Mandan and Hidatsa villages

With Lewis on his stomach in the pirogue, the Corps pushed off to the east. When they were coming upstream, the explorers had struggled to travel 15 miles a day against the powerful Missouri River. Now the river helped them along. They raced downstream. Within days they reached the villages of the Mandan and Hidatsa tribes.

The explorers fired their guns in greeting as they approached the first village. People along the shore shouted a hearty welcome. It was good to be among friends again. They made camp near Black Cat's lodge, where Lewis could rest and recover. The people of the village gathered to welcome them and hear their stories. Captain Clark and Chief Black Cat sat together to talk and smoke a pipe.

Children ran between the lodges, shouting and laughing as they played follow the leader. Others splashed and swam in the river. Women tended their gardens. The corn grew tall and sunflowers turned their heads to follow the path of the sun as it crossed the sky. Young men galloped off on their horses in hunting parties. The women skinned, carved, and cooked the buffalo they caught.

While Lewis recovered, Clark held talks with the chiefs of the tribe. He asked if some among them would travel east with the Corps to visit with the "Great Father," President Jefferson. The Indians were reluctant, but one chief, Big White, agreed to make the journey east with his wife and son.

Just as Big White agreed to go east, one of the Corps's members decided to turn back to the west. Private John Colter had made friends with the fur traders Dickson and Hancock, and they had asked him to join them in their venture. Colter asked the captains if he could resign from the Corps. He wasn't ready to return to the cities of the east—he'd be "lonely" there, he said. The west had captured his spirit. The captains agreed to let him go. They thanked him and gave him enough tools and ammunition to keep him supplied for two years.

It was hard to say good-bye to a member of their company. The years and their long journey had created a strong bond. It was time, too, to say good-bye to three other companions—Charbonneau, Sacagawea, and Pomp. This was their home. Clark, especially, was torn at the thought of leaving little Pomp. He'd grown to love the "butifull promising child." He made an offer to Charbonneau and Sacagawea to take little Pomp and raise him as his own, and to see that he received an education. The baby's parents were pleased by the offer and agreed to bring Pomp to St. Louis when he was old enough. Clark left them, sad but hopeful that he would once again see the little dancing boy.

Lewis was beginning to recover. It was time to move on. The captains had one last pipe with the chiefs of the villages. If they weren't so eager to get home, the parting would have been terribly sad. As it was, they left with mixed emotions. Many of the people cried out when Big White and his family climbed into one of the boats. They were uneasy as they watched their chief leave for lands unknown, and they worried that they would never see him again.

The men of the Corps couldn't wait to get back home. They sped past camps and landmarks they remembered vividly from their trip up the river. They stopped briefly at the Arikara villages.

A Mandan village

Celebrate 200 Years!

The bicentennial (200th anniversary) of the Lewis and Clark Expedition will be a three-year celebration, from 2003 to 2006. Thanks to the National Park Service, state agencies, and the Lewis and Clark Trail Heritage Foundation, the route of the expedition can be followed from St. Louis to the Pacific Ocean. You can honor the bicentennial by camping along or visiting some portion of the Lewis and Clark National Historic Trail. Here are some special places that might be close to your home (more information on these sites and others can be found at the end of this book):

The Museum of Western Expansion and the Jefferson National Expansion Memorial in St. Louis marks the beginning of the expedition's journey up the Missouri River.

Lewis and Clark State Park in Onawa, Iowa, has a replica of the *Discovery*. In Sioux City, Iowa, visit Sergeant Floyd's Monument.

In Washburn, North Dakota, you can explore the excellent Lewis and Clark Interpretive Center and see the reconstructed Fort Mandan, where the Corps wintered with the Mandan and Hidatsa people. Nearby Knife River Indian Villages National Historic Site was the home of Sacagawea.

You'll want to spend whole days at the Lewis and Clark National Historic Trail Interpretive Center in Great Falls, Montana, where interactive exhibits describe the entire journey.

Camp at the Missouri Headwaters State Park near Bozeman, Montana, where Sacagawea was captured by Hidatsa Indians, and where three rivers merge to form the Missouri River. In Billings, Montana, you can see Clark's signature carved on Pompey's Pillar.

The Nez Perce National Historical Park based in Spalding, Idaho, features 24 sites important to the Nez Perce people.

Camp at Beacon Rock State Park along the Columbia River, and see artifacts at the Columbia Gorge Discovery Center in The Dalles, Oregon, and the Columbia Gorge Interpretive Center in Stevenson, Washington.

If you live on the west coast, you can stop at Fort Canby State Park in Ilwaco, Washington, for the ocean view and interpretive center, and Fort Clatsop National Memorial where the reconstructed winter fort is full of period clothing and supplies.

You can also see reenactors at one of the many Lewis and Clark festivals held throughout the country

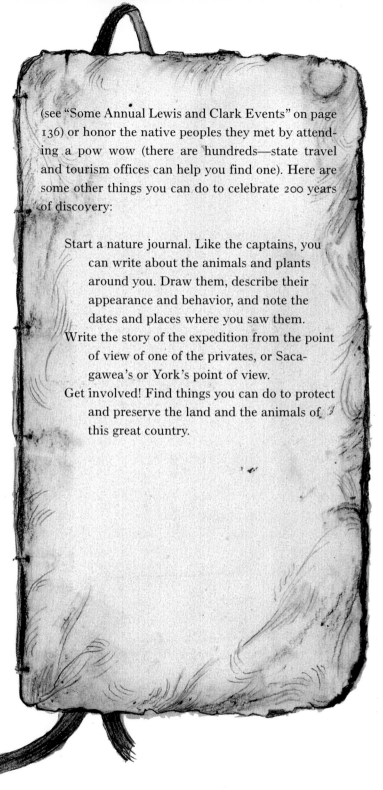

(see "Some Annual Lewis and Clark Events" on page 136) or honor the native peoples they met by attending a pow wow (there are hundreds—state travel and tourism offices can help you find one). Here are some other things you can do to celebrate 200 years of discovery:

Start a nature journal. Like the captains, you can write about the animals and plants around you. Draw them, describe their appearance and behavior, and note the dates and places where you saw them.

Write the story of the expedition from the point of view of one of the privates, or Sacagawea's or York's point of view.

Get involved! Find things you can do to protect and preserve the land and the animals of this great country.

They didn't stop when they saw dozens of armed Teton Sioux along the banks or when Black Buffalo shouted to them from a hill. At Floyd's Bluff they paused to say good-bye to the one member of the Corps who did not survive the journey. How long ago it seemed that they had stood at this place. They were traveling from 50 to 80 miles a day. Distances that had taken them months to cover going west were now crossed in days. The men rowed with all their will and strength.

As they traveled downstream, they met several voyagers making their way up. Traders were bringing goods to barter with the Sioux. Other groups were going west to trap beaver. It was amazing to hear news from the cities of the east, a world they had heard nothing about for over two years. Another exploratory mission had left for the west— Zebulon Pike had set out from St. Louis on a journey through the southwest and into the Rocky Mountains. There had been another election and Thomas Jefferson was still president. Everyone gathered around to hear the amazing story of the duel between Vice President Aaron Burr and Federalist Party leader Alexander Hamilton.

The traders and trappers were equally amazed to see the Corps of Discovery. The country had long ago given up hope that the men would return from their journey. The captains exchanged corn for flour and tobacco from one trader while their men exchanged their ragged buckskins for the traders' cleaner clothes. Others gave the explorers gifts of whiskey and chocolate. The traders asked and customs. They'd discovered and mapped rivers, mountains, and plains. They'd observed and described 122 animal species and 178 species of plants. They had forged a passage across the great continent and reached the vast Pacific Ocean.

September 21, 1806
The Corps reaches St. Charles

As Lewis's mind went back over the events of the past two years, the men pulled the boats forward toward home. "The party being extreemly anxious to get down [river] ply their ores very well," wrote Clark. Everyone was so anxious to reach St. Louis that they agreed to stop hunting and lived on fruit they picked hurriedly along the riverbanks. One day they saw a cow and shouted with joy at this four-footed sign of civilization. They passed a tiny settlement, La Charrette, whose residents were stunned at the sight of the Corps. Farther downstream, they approached St. Charles, the village they'd left two years and four months before. As they came close to the village, they shot their guns in salute. The villagers raced from their cabins to watch as the strange fleet landed on the shore. There was much rejoicing and astonishment. The explorers were given a great welcome, food and drink, and beds to sleep in that night.

Plains Indian hunting shirt collected by Lewis and Clark

them endless questions about their adventures in the west. They stayed up late at night swapping stories and singing loud songs with their countrymen.

By now Captain Lewis was completely recovered. He was once again able to walk—and sit! He began to write a report on their journey for President Jefferson. There was so much to say! They'd met dozens of Indian tribes and studied their languages

September 23, 1806
The Corps is back in St. Louis

Days later the Corps pulled its boats into the Mississippi River. The explorers paddled past their old barracks at Camp Wood and eagerly approached the town of St. Louis. Again, they fired their guns in salute. Their arrival turned the town upside down with excitement. Everyone gathered to welcome the long-lost heroes. The explorers, who had conquered the challenge of the crossing and had seen the continent, were looked upon with awe.

Their welcome home could not have been better. They were entertained and toasted. Feasts and dances were held in their honor. After more than two years and 8,000 miles, the Corps was home again. The men, from young George Shannon and the brothers Joseph and Reuben Field, to Pierre Cruzatte, George Drouillard, York, and their bold captains Meriwether Lewis and William Clark, were heroes. Even Seaman had earned a place in history.

Lewis sent a letter to President Jefferson to tell him of their safe return. "In obedience to your orders," he wrote, "we have penitrated the continent of North America to the Pacific Ocean." On hearing of their return Jefferson felt "unspeakable joy." Not since the keelboat had come back downriver had he heard from his friend Lewis. The long-held dream of crossing the continent had been fulfilled. President Jefferson couldn't wait to hear every detail of the journey.

After a short rest the captains and several of the men left for the east with Big White and his family. When they reached Kentucky, Clark remained behind to see his family, then he moved on to Virginia on an important mission. There was a young woman in Virginia for whom a river far off in the western lands was named. Clark proposed to the woman, Julia Hancock, and she happily accepted. Lewis took Mandan chief Big White to Wash-

ington, where President Jefferson held a great celebration to honor his Indian visitors and the bold explorers.

The men of the Corps of Discovery were honored by Congress with rewards of land and money. York, as a slave, was not rewarded, but eventually Clark granted him his freedom. Clark gave him a wagon and a team of horses that York used to start up a freight-hauling business. The first black man to cross the land that was to become the continental United States, York died in 1832.

Others went back to their lives, made richer by their experiences and rewards. Sergeant John Ordway settled down, married, and published his journal of the expedition. Young George Shannon was one of the men assigned to bring Big White back to his village. A surprise attack by an Arikara band turned them back. Shannon lost his leg in the battle, but that didn't stop him from building a successful career in politics. Another man on this mission, Nathaniel Pryor, served in the War of 1812, then married an Osage woman and went to live with her tribe. Big White returned home, but not for two more years.

John Colter, who had remained in the west, discovered amazing new lands and had many more adventures. Another of the men, John Potts, went back to join him. As they camped near the Three Forks of the Missouri River, they were attacked by Blackfoot Indians, and Potts was killed. The warriors stripped Colter and gave him a chance to run. He bolted away. One of the Indians caught up with him, but Colter grabbed his spear and killed him. Colter then jumped into a river and hid from the rest of the warriors. Naked and alone, he walked for miles until finally, seven days later, he came to a

trapper's cabin. Colter eventually settled down in the little community of La Charrette and married.

George Drouillard went west and was killed as he trapped beaver near the headwaters of the Missouri River. Pierre Cruzatte also met his death at the hands of the Blackfoot Indians. Patrick Gass, who had been promoted to sergeant after Floyd's death, lived to be 99 years old. At age 90, when the Civil War broke out, he volunteered to fight for the Union army. (The Union politely refused his services.) Gass's journal of the expedition's journey was also published.

Charbonneau, too, lived to an old age. A few years after the expedition, he and Sacagawea brought Pomp and his new little sister, Lizette, downriver to St. Louis. There Clark was happy to fulfill the promise he'd made to them. He paid for Pomp's schooling and became Lizette's guardian. He made a gift of land to Charbonneau. For a while Charbonneau and Sacagawea farmed the plot of land, but they missed their life on the plains and eventually left to make their way back home. Sacagawea died in 1812 at a fort on the Missouri River.

Sacagawea's son, no longer the child Pomp but the man Jean Baptiste, finished his education. He befriended a visiting German prince who had an interest in American Indians. He traveled to Europe with the prince, staying for five years and learning four languages. On his return he went back to the west and became an interpreter, guide, trapper, and gold-miner.

Captains Lewis and Clark received rewards of land, money, and great acclaim. Meriwether Lewis was designated Governor of the Louisiana Territory; William Clark became Brigadier General of Militia and Superintendent of Indian Affairs for the Louisiana Territory.

Lewis's life after the expedition went into a downward spiral. He suffered from complicated financial problems and the many challenges of his new position. Always a moody person, Lewis began to show signs of deeper problems. When the government questioned the expenses he had approved to bring Big White back to his village, it added to his burdens. He gathered his things and left St. Louis to go to Washington to defend his decisions.

Lewis boarded a riverboat and went downstream to Memphis. From there he traveled on horseback along a dark, forested trail, the Natchez Trace, on his way to the east. One day he arrived at an inn called Grinder's Stand and took a cabin for the night. In the dark of the night Mrs. Grinder was awakened by the sound of two gunshots. Her guest, the esteemed Meriwether Lewis, was terribly wounded, and a few hours later he died. Most historians believe that Lewis, burdened and depressed, took his own life. Some believe that he was the victim of bandits, not an unlikely possibility along the dark and dangerous Natchez Trace.

Clark was brokenhearted by the loss of his worthy friend Lewis. Their friendship, forged when they were young men in the army, had grown stronger on their great journey. Clark named his eldest son Meriwether Lewis Clark.

A Dakota chief

Clark went on to accomplish many things. He was fair and just in his position as head of Indian affairs. The native people he worked with respected and liked him. They called him the "Red-Hair Chief." Clark became Governor of the Missouri

Territory and created a museum of natural history and Indian artifacts. He had six sons and a daughter in addition to his relationship with Jean Baptiste and Lizette. His journals and those of his dear friend Lewis were published, and the story of their great journey is still told today.

How often in later years did Clark stand on the banks of the Missouri River and look west? How many times did he close his eyes and imagine the vast plains, the tall grasses swaying in the wind, and the herds of buffalo that dotted the countryside? Did he see the bold dance of the Sioux warriors in the flickering firelight? Did he hear the yelps of prairie dogs, the lonely sounds of howling wolves? Perhaps he relived the moment when, cold and wet, he saw the wide Pacific Ocean. Maybe he smiled remembering Pomp dancing by the warm light of a campfire. What marvels he and Lewis had seen. Clark must have wished many times to be back in camp writing in his journal of the day's adventures—"We set out early under a gentle breeze . . ."

Glossary

BUCKSKIN The tanned skin of a deer

BULLBOAT A small round boat made of buffalo hides stretched over willow branches

BURIAL SCAFFOLD Raised wooden structure on which some tribes placed their dead

CACHE Hidden or stored provisions; the act of burying or hiding the supplies

CAPSIZE To upset or overturn

CORPS In the military, a unit between a division and an army; in the case of the Corps of Discovery, it refers to a number of persons working together to reach a goal

COUNT COUP To strike an enemy with one's hands or with a special stick.

CRADLEBOARD A carrier for a baby made of a wrapper of animal skin attached to a stiff piece of rawhide or a wood frame

DUGOUT A canoe made of a hollowed-out log

EARTH LODGE Homes of timber covered with earth common to several tribes along the upper Missouri River

ESPONTOON A long staff with a metal tip, used as a spear

GAUNTLET (ALSO SPELLED "GANTLET") A punishment in which the lawbreaker ran between two lines of men who struck him as he passed

GREAT PLAINS A large area of North America, west of the Missouri and Mississippi Rivers and east of the Rocky Mountains, ranging from Canada to New Mexico and Texas, noted for open, mostly treeless grasslands, low rainfall, and harsh weather conditions

HABITAT The natural environment of an animal, plant, or other species

KEELBOAT A large, shallow boat generally used to haul freight

LEGGINGS Covering for the legs made of animal skin

MEDICINE In North American Indian cultures, this word refers to spiritual powers possessed by things or people

MEDICINE BUNDLE Sacred objects collected by an individual that are symbolic of the power of his or her spirit guide

NOMADIC Moving from place to place

PELT Untanned animal skin that has hair, wool, or fur

PEMMICAN Meat that is cut into strips, pounded into a paste with fat and berries, and dried

PIROGUE A flat-bottomed canoe made from a hollowed-out log

PISHKUN A buffalo jump; a cliff where buffalo were herded to their deaths

PLAINS See Great Plains

PORTAGE To transport boats and supplies overland from a river or lake to another body of water; the route over which the transporting is done

PREDATOR An animal that eats other animals

PREY An animal that is hunted by other animals

RAWHIDE Untanned animal skin

SPECIES A category of plants or animals that share some common characteristics and are designated by a common name

SWEETGRASS A long grass that grows in the northern plains

TALLOW Animal fat

TAN The process of treating hides or skins to make them into leather

TIPI (ALSO SPELLED "TEPEE") A cone-shaped tent, the traditional lodging of nomadic Indians of the Great Plains, made of animal skins and poles

TRAVOIS A sled made of two poles that is dragged by a horse or dog

VOYAGERS (FRENCH SPELLING IS "VOYAGEURS") French-Canadian boatmen or fur traders who were often employed by trading companies to take men and supplies to remote trading posts

Lewis and Clark Sites, Organizations, and Events

(Addresses and numbers listed are for further information.)

BIG BONE LICK STATE PARK

See fossil displays, a life-size model of a mastodon, and a live herd of buffalo.

3380 Beaver Road, Union, Kentucky 41091-9627, 606-384-3522

THE MUSEUM OF WESTERN EXPANSION/JEFFERSON NATIONAL EXPANSION MEMORIAL

Learn about the explorers and pioneers who followed President Jefferson's vision—then ride a tram to the top of the Gateway Arch.

11 N. 4th Street, St. Louis, Missouri 63102, 314-655-1600

LEWIS & CLARK CENTER

Dioramas tell the story of the journey of the Corps of Discovery.

701 Riverside Drive, St. Charles, Missouri 63304, 314-947-3199

JOSLYN ART MUSEUM

See paintings by artists who traveled up the Missouri River in the 1800s.

2200 Dodge Street, Omaha, Nebraska 68102-1292, 402-342-3300

LEWIS AND CLARK STATE PARK

This park features replicas of the *Discovery* and the expedition's pirogues.

21914 Park Loop, Onawa, Iowa 51040, 712-423-2829

SERGEANT FLOYD'S MONUMENT

Sergeant Charles Floyd, the only explorer who died during the expedition, is buried here.

1000 Larsen Park Road, Sioux City, Iowa 51103

SIOUX CITY PUBLIC MUSEUM

See exhibits on Plains and Woodland tribes as well as wildlife of the region.

2901 Jackson Street, Sioux City, Iowa 51104, 712-279-6174

AKTA LAKOTA MUSEUM

Learn about the Lakota through their arts and crafts.

St. Joseph Indian School, North Main Street, Chamberlain, South Dakota 57325, 605-734-3452

MUSEUM OF THE SOUTH DAKOTA STATE HISTORICAL SOCIETY

The Oyate Tawicoh'an (The Ways of the People) exhibit focuses on the customs of Plains Indians.

900 Governors Drive, Pierre, South Dakota 57501, 605-773-3458

FORT PIERRE NATIONAL GRASSLAND

See what a real prairie is like!

124 S. Euclid Street, Pierre, South Dakota 57501, 695-224-5517

FORT ABRAHAM LINCOLN STATE PARK

Visit the reconstructed Mandan On-A-Slant Village.

Bismarck Mandan Visitors Bureau, 523 N. Fourth Street, Bismarck, North Dakota, 58501, 701-222-4308

NORTH DAKOTA HERITAGE CENTER

Amazing artifacts of many Plains tribes.

612 East Boulevard Avenue, Bismarck, North Dakota 58501, 701-224-2666

LEWIS AND CLARK INTERPRETIVE CENTER

Try on a buffalo robe, listen to Mandan drums, and visit the reconstructed Fort Mandan nearby.

North Dakota Lewis and Clark Bicentennial Foundation, Box 607, Washburn, North Dakota 58577, 701-462-8535

CROSS RANCH NATURE PRESERVE

Thanks to the Nature Conservancy you can walk in country that is still like it was when the expedition came this way. Buffalo live here!

Cross Ranch Nature Preserve, H.C.I. Box 112, Hensler, North Dakota 58547, 701-794-3731

KNIFE RIVER INDIAN VILLAGES NATIONAL HISTORIC SITE

This Hidatsa site is the one-time home of Sacagawea; see ancient caches, travois trails, and earth lodges.

Box 9, Stanton, North Dakota 58571-0009, 701-745-3309

THREE AFFILIATED TRIBES MUSEUM

The Mandan, Hidatsa, and Arikara tribes are now the Three Affiliated Tribes. Their museum features tools, clothing, and other artifacts as well as crafts made by the people of the reservation.

Highway 23, Fort Berthold Reservation 98763, 701-627-4477

FORT UNION TRADING POST NATIONAL HISTORIC SITE

Stand at the junction of the Yellowstone and Missouri Rivers.

Rural Route 3, Box 71, Williston, North Dakota 58801-9455, 701-572-9083

ULM PISHKUN STATE PARK

This prehistoric pishkun (buffalo jump) is considered the largest in the United States.

342 Ulm Vaughn Road, Ulm, Montana 59485, 406-454-5840

LEWIS AND CLARK NATIONAL HISTORIC TRAIL INTERPRETIVE CENTER

Try your hand at pulling a pirogue upriver. Listen to Lewis's request for horses as it is translated from English to French to Hidatsa to the Shoshone language. Enjoy the many other interactive exhibits at this museum located near the Great Falls camp.

P.O. Box 1806, Great Falls, Montana 59403, 406-727-8733

MISSOURI HEADWATERS STATE PARK

Stand at the place where the Jefferson, Gallatin, and Madison Rivers combine to form the Missouri River.

Montana Fish, Wildlife & Parks, 1400 South 19th, Bozeman, Montana 59715, 406-994-4042

POMPEY'S PILLAR NATIONAL HISTORIC LANDMARK

See Clark's signature in stone.

810 East Main Street, Billings, Montana 59105-3395, 406-875-2233

NEZ PERCE NATIONAL HISTORICAL PARK

One of the park's 24 sites shows where the Corps camped in spring 1806. The visitor center displays a dugout canoe and an original Jefferson peace medal.

Route 1, Box 100, Highway 95, Spalding, Idaho 83540, 208-843-2261

SACAJAWEA STATE PARK

Displays on Sacagawea's contributions and artifacts of northwest tribes.

Highway 12, Pasco, Washington 99301, 509-545-2361

BEACON ROCK STATE PARK

Get in shape—you'll want to hike to the top of Beacon Rock for a view of the Columbia River.

Stevenson, Washington, on Highway 14, 509-427-8265

COLUMBIA GORGE DISCOVERY CENTER

See an espontoon and other tools the expedition used, as well as exhibits on people and animals of the Columbia River.

Discovery Drive, The Dalles, Oregon 97338, 541-296-8600

Fort Clatsop National Memorial

Interpreters at reconstructed Fort Clatsop carve dugouts, smoke meat, and make candles just like the members of the expedition. An interpretive center includes artifacts of Pacific Northwest tribes. You can also visit the nearby Salt Camp.

92343 Fort Clatsop Road, Astoria, Oregon 97103, 503-861-2471

Columbia Gorge Interpretive Center

Learn about the people of the Columbia River through the thousands of artifacts and photographs displayed here.

990 S.W. Rock Creek Drive, Stevenson, Washington 98648, 509-427-8211

Fort Canby State Park

Walk to the ocean and pretend you've spent a year and a half getting there! Follow the trail from St. Louis to the ocean at the interpretive center, where you can see a pirogue and items belonging to Corps members.

Box 488, Robert Gray Drive, Ilwaco, Washington 98624, 360-642-3078

Organizations

National Park Service

Follow the trail! Contact the National Park Service for booklets and information on the Lewis and Clark National Historic Trail.

1709 Jackson Street, Omaha, Nebraska 68102, 402-221-3471, www.nps.gov/lecl

Lewis and Clark Trail Heritage Foundation

A nonprofit organization dedicated to the preservation of the heritage of the Lewis and Clark Expedition. Members work with the National Park Service to help preserve and interpret the Lewis and Clark National Historic Trail. The Foundation organizes programs and special events, coordinates volunteer projects, and publishes a quarterly journal, *We Proceeded On*.

P.O. Box 3434, Great Falls, Montana 59403, www.lewisandclarktrail.com/

Annual Lewis and Clark Events

Lewis and Clark Rendezvous (May)

230 S. Main Street, St. Charles, Missouri 63301, 800-366-2427 or 314-946-7776

Lewis and Clark Festival (June)

Lewis and Clark State Park, 21914 Park Loop, Onawa, Iowa 51040, 712-423-2829

North Dakota Lewis and Clark Days (June)

North Dakota Lewis and Clark Bicentennial Foundation, P.O. Box 607, Washburn, North Dakota 58577, 701-462-8535

Annual Lewis and Clark Festival (July)

Great Falls Convention and Visitors Bureau, P.O. Box 2127, Great Falls, Montana 59403, 406-761-1888

Lewis and Clark Days Festival (July)

Chamberlain Area Chamber of Commerce, P.O. Box 517, Chamberlain, South Dakota, 57325 605-734-6541

Lewis and Clark Festival (August)

Yankton Area Chamber of Commerce, P.O. Box 588D, Yankton, South Dakota, 57078, 800-888-1460 or 402-667-7873

Web Sites to Explore

MONTICELLO, HOME OF THOMAS JEFFERSON

www.monticello.org

Follow Thomas Jefferson through a day in his life at Monticello. You can even ask Thomas Jefferson a question!

LEWIS & CLARK ON THE INFORMATION SUPERHIGHWAY

www.vpds.wsu.edu/lcexpedition/resources

A long list of links—everything you ever wanted to know about the Lewis and Clark Expedition.

KEELBOATS

www.keelboat.com/kb1.htm

See photos of a replica keelboat under construction.

LEWIS AND CLARK'S CORPS OF DISCOVERY: GREAT FALLS, MONTANA

www.corpsofdiscovery.org/honor.htm

See reenactors making a dugout canoe.

THE JOURNEY OF THE CORPS OF THE DISCOVERY

www.pbs.org/lewisandclark

Read biographies of all the members of the expedition, get a Lewis and Clark screensaver, read the captains' journals, and participate in an interactive story—you lead the expedition!

PEABODY MUSEUM OF ARCHAEOLOGY AND ETHNOLOGY AT HARVARD UNIVERSITY

www.peabody.harvard.edu/Lewis&Clark

See objects brought back from the west by Lewis and Clark, including a Mandan buffalo robe, a Clatsop hat, and an otter skin pouch.

GEOGRAPHIC NAME SERVER

www.mit.edu/geo

Find latitude and longitude locations for U.S. cities, then go to . . .

HOW FAR IS IT?

www.indo.com/distance/

To calculate distances between cities.

U.S. GEOLOGICAL SURVEY'S VOLCANO OBSERVATORY

vulcan.wr.usgs.gov/

See photos of Mount St. Helens before, during, and after the explosion. "Volcanocam" shows a live view of Mount St. Helens today.

ASK A QUESTION

www.cr.nps.gov/history/askhist.htm

National Park Service historians are available here to answer your questions.

NATIONAL PARK SERVICE'S LEWIS AND CLARK NATIONAL HISTORIC TRAIL HOME PAGE

www.nps.gov/lecl/

Go here for news and information on the trail today. Click on the trail sites to learn more. The informative pages of the Knife River Indian Village National Historic Site tell how the Mandan and Hidatsa people lived.

NATIVE AMERICAN CULTURE

www.greatdreams.com/native.htm

Here's a site on hundreds of Native American tribes, including history, stories, interviews, art, and information on visiting reservations.

AMERICAN INDIANS AND THE NATURAL WORLD

www.clpgh.org/cmnh/exhibits/north-south-east-west/index.html

This site of the Carnegie Museum of Natural History tells how native people from the four corners of the United States share the earth with others.

THE SALMON PAGE

www.riverdale.k12.or.us/salmon.htm

Learn about students saving salmon, get salmon trivia, and follow links to dozens of excellent, informative sites.

ENDANGERED SPECIES

www.endangeredspecie.com/kids.htm

Learn about endangered species.

NATIONAL WILDLIFE FEDERATION'S ANIMAL TRACKS

www.nwf.org/nwf/kids/

Enjoy games and habitat tours, and find information about different animals. Check in with Ranger Rick for help with homework and tips for saving the planet.

DISCOVERY CHANNEL'S OTTER SITE

www.discovery.com/stories/nature/otters/otters.html

Learn how people are working to help otters.

INTERTRIBAL BISON COOPERATIVE—TRADITIONAL USES OF THE BUFFALO

www.intertribalbison.org/fun.htm

A page of bison fun. Click on different parts of the buffalo to learn what Indians made from its gifts. The 42 tribes of the Intertribal Bison Cooperative are working to return the buffalo to Indian country.

NATIONAL GEOGRAPHIC'S UNDERDOGS: PRAIRIE DOGS AT HOME

www.nationalgeographic.com/features/98/burrow

Enter a prairie dog tunnel and find out about their secret underground lives.

THE BEAR DEN

www.nature-net.com/bears

Links and information about grizzly bears and other bears. Stop by the Cub Den, too.

WOLVES ON THE WEB

www.wolves-on-web.com

Click to hear wolves howling, see pictures, read stories, learn facts about wolves, and read the latest news on rescue efforts.

Bibliography

Ambrose, Stephen E. *Undaunted Courage: Meriwether Lewis, Thomas Jefferson, and the Opening of the American West*. New York: Touchstone Books, 1996.

Anderson, Irving, W. "Sacajawea? Sakakawea? Scagawea?" *We Proceeded On* (Summer 1975).

Bakeless, John, editor. *The Journals of Lewis and Clark*. New York: New American Library, 1964.

Burns, Ken, executive producer, and Dayton Duncan, producer and writer. *Lewis & Clark: The Journey of the Corps of Discovery*. 1997.

Catlin, George. *North American Indians*. New York: Penguin Books, 1989.

Collins, Henry Hill Jr. *Complete Field Guide to North American Wildlife*. New York: Harper & Row, 1981.

Cutright, Paul Russell. *Lewis and Clark: Pioneering Naturalists*. Urbana, IL: University of Illinois Press, 1969.

DeVoto, Bernard, ed. *The Journals of Lewis and Clark*. New York: Houghton Mifflin Company, 1997.

Flaherty, Thomas H. *The Buffalo Hunters*. Alexandria, VA: Time-Life Books, 1993.

Fronval, George and Daniel Dubois. *Indian Signals and Sign Language*. Avenel, NJ: Wings Books, 1978.*

Goodchild, Peter. *Survival Skills of the North American Indians*. Chicago: Chicago Review Press, 1999.

Hofsinde, Robert. *Indian Sign Language*. New York: William Morrow & Co., 1956.

Hoover, Herbert T. *The Yankton Sioux*. New York: Chelsea House Publishers, 1988.*

Murie, Olaus J. *A Field Guide to Animal Tracks*. Boston: Houghton Mifflin Company, 1975.

Papanek, John L. *Cycles of Life*. Alexandria, VA: Time-Life Books, 1994.

Robbins, Chandler, et al. *Birds of North America*. New York: Golden Press, 1966.

Sandoz, Mari. *These Were the Sioux*. Lincoln, NE: University of Nebraska Press, 1961.*

Snyder, Gerald S. *In the Footsteps of Lewis and Clark*. Washington D.C.: National Geographic Society, 1970.

Solomon, Eldra, et al. *Biology*. Fort Worth, TX: Harcourt Brace College Publishers, 1996.

Taylor, Colin F., ed. *The Native Americans: The Indigenous People of North America*. New York: Smithmark Publishers, 1992.

Waldman, Carl. *Atlas of the North American Indian*. New York: Facts On File, Inc., 1985.

Yue, David and Charlotte Yue. *The Tipi: A Center of Native American Life*. New York: Alfred A. Knopf, 1984.*

*These books are especially recommended for children.

Photo Credits

Time Line

p. xii (top) Meriwether Lewis, Charles Willson Peale, 1807. Courtesy of Independence National Historical Park, Philadelphia, PA. (middle) William Clark, Charles Willson Peale, 1807. Courtesy of Independence National Historical Park, Philadelphia, PA. (bottom) Thomas Jefferson, Charles Willson Peale, 1807. Courtesy of Independence National Historical Park, Philadelphia, PA. *Map of Lewis and Clark's Track across the Western Portion of North American, from the Mississippi to the Pacific Ocean.* Courtesy of the National Archives.

p. xiii (left) *Lewis and Clark at St. Charles, May 21, 1804.* Charles Morganthaler. Courtesy of the St. Charles County Historical Society. (right) William Clark's elkskin-bound journal. Courtesy of the Missouri Historical Society.

Preface

p. xvii Thomas Jefferson, Charles Willson Peale, 1807. Courtesy of Independence National Historical Park, Philadelphia, PA.

Time Line of the Lewis and Clark Expedition

p. xviii (lower left) *View on the Missouri, Alluvial Banks Falling in, 600 Miles above St. Louis.* George Catlin, 1832. Courtesy of National Museum of American Art, Smithsonian Institution. Gift of Mrs. Joseph Harrison, Jr. (upper right) *View from Floyd's Grave, 1,000 Miles above St. Louis.* George Catlin, 1832. Courtesy of National Museum of American Art, Smithsonian Institution. Gift of Mrs. Joseph Harrison, Jr.

p. xix (lower left) *Lewis and Clark at Three Forks.* Edgar S. Paxson. Mural in the Montana State Capital. Courtesy of the Montana Historical Society. (upper right) *Lewis and Clark Entering Mandan Village.* R. W. Smith, oil. Courtesy of the State Historical Society of North Dakota.

Chapter 1

p. 2 Meriwether Lewis, Charles Willson Peale, 1807. Courtesy of Independence National Historical Park, Philadelphia, PA.

p. 4 William Clark, Charles Willson Peale, 1807. Courtesy of Independence National Historical Park, Philadelphia, PA.

p. 9 *Lewis and Clark at St. Charles, May 21, 1804.* Charles Morganthaler. Courtesy of the St. Charles County Historical Society.

p. 11 *View on the Missouri, Alluvial Banks Falling in, 600 Miles above St. Louis.* George Catlin, 1832. Courtesy of National Museum of American Art, Smithsonian Institution. Gift of Mrs. Joseph Harrison, Jr.

Chapter 2

p. 18 William Clark's elkskin-bound journal. Courtesy of the Missouri Historical Society.

p. 19 *Missouri River Travelers Camp.* Karl Bodmer, 1839–1843, engraving and aquatint. Courtesy of the State Historical Society of North Dakota.

p. 25 *View from Floyd's Grave, 1,000 Miles above St. Louis.* George Catlin, 1832. Courtesy of National Museum of American Art, Smithsonian Institution. Gift of Mrs. Joseph Harrison, Jr.

p. 27 *Lewis and Clark Crossing South Dakota in 1804.* Courtesy of the Missouri Historical Society.

p. 28 *Buffalo Cow Grazing on the Prairie.* George Catlin, 1832–1833. Courtesy of National Museum of American Art, Smithsonian Institution. Gift of Mrs. Joseph Harrison, Jr.

Chapter 3

p. 30 (middle) Rain-in-the-face, a Hunkpapa Sioux. Courtesy of the National Archives.

p. 30 (left) *Teton Sioux horse races in front of Fort Pierre, South Dakota.* Karl Bodmer, 1833–34. Courtesy of the National Archives.

p. 31 Medicine bags, Edward S. Curtis. Courtesy of the Edward S. Curtis Archives.

p. 35 Moving camp, Edward S. Curtis. Courtesy of the Edward S. Curtis Archives.

p. 41 *Great Camp of the Piekanns near Fort McKenzie, Montana.* Karl Bodmer, 1833. Courtesy of the National Archives.

p. 43 *York.* Charles M. Russell, watercolor, 1908. Courtesy of the Montana Historical Society, gift of the artist.

p. 45 (detail) *Mandan Village.* Karl Bodmer, 1839–1843, engraving and aquatint. Courtesy of the State Historical Society of North Dakota.

Chapter 4

p. 48 *Lewis and Clark Entering Mandan Village.* R. W. Smith, oil. Courtesy of the State Historical Society of North Dakota.

p. 49 Replica of Fort Mandan near Washburn, North Dakota. Courtesy of the North Dakota Lewis & Clark Bicentennial Foundation.

p. 52 *Pehriska-Ruhpa, in the Costume of the Dog Band of the Hidatsa.* Karl Bodmer, 1833–34. Courtesy of the National Archives.

p. 53 *Pawnee Lodges at Loup, Nebraska, with a Family Standing in front of a Lodge Entrance.* William H. Jackson. Courtesy of the National Archives.

p. 54 *Mandan Earth Lodge.* Karl Bodmer, 1839–1843, engraving and aquatint. Courtesy of the State Historical Society of North Dakota.

Index

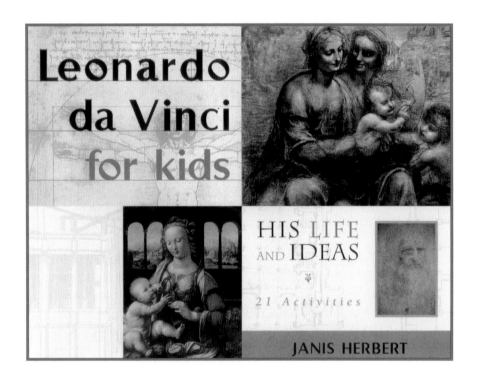
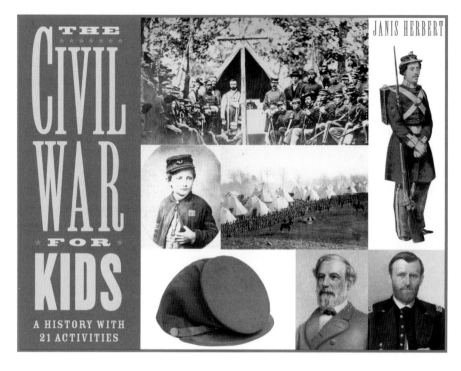